THE ROME ADVENTURE: A TRAVEL PREPARATION GUIDE

SHONDA WILLIAMS

Table Of Contents

Introduction

Rome is one of the most fascinating cities in the world, with a rich history, culture, and art that spans over two millennia. Rome has something for you, whether you are interested in ancient ruins, Renaissance masterpieces, Baroque fountains, or modern cuisine. In this travel guide, you will find everything you need to know to plan your perfect trip to the Eternal City.

Rome is divided into several districts, each with its character and attractions. The historic centre (Centro Storico) is where you will find the most famous landmarks, such as the Colosseum, the Roman Forum, the Pantheon, and the Trevi Fountain. This area is also home to many museums, churches, palaces, and squares that showcase the artistic and architectural heritage of Rome. You can easily explore this district on foot or by public transport, as it is well connected by buses and metro lines.

Another district that you should not miss is Vatican City, the smallest sovereign state in the world and the seat of the Catholic Church. Here you can admire the stunning St. Peter's Basilica, the largest church in the world, and the magnificent Vatican Museums, where you can see the Sistine Chapel and its famous frescoes by Michelangelo. Vatican City is also a place of pilgrimage for millions of faithful who come to see the Pope and attend his weekly audiences.

To experience the lively and colourful side of Rome, you should visit Trastevere, a charming neighbourhood on the west bank of the Tiber River. This area is known for its narrow cobblestone streets, medieval houses, quaint shops, and cosy restaurants. Trastevere is also a popular nightlife spot, where you can enjoy live music, street performers, and local bars.

Rome is not only a city of art and history, but also a city of food and wine. You will be spoiled for choice when it comes to dining in Rome, as there are countless options for every taste and budget. You can try traditional Roman cuisine, based on simple ingredients such as pasta, cheese, meat, and vegetables. Some of the most famous dishes are carbonara, amatriciana, cacio e pepe, and saltimbocca. You can also sample the delicious pizza, gelato, coffee, and pastries that Rome has to offer. Rome is a city that will surprise you with its diversity and charm. No matter how long you stay or how many times you visit, you will always find something new and exciting to discover. This travel guide will help you make the most of your time in Rome and enjoy its unforgettable attractions. Buon viaggio!

Chapter 1 • Welcome to Rome

Brief History of Rome

Rome is a city that has witnessed the rise and fall of empires, the birth and spread of religions, and the creation and destruction of art. Its history is a fascinating and complex story that spans over 2,500 years.

Rome was founded in 753 BC by Romulus and Remus, twin brothers who were descendants of the Trojan hero,

Aeneas. They were raised by a she-wolf after being abandoned by their uncle, the king of Alba Longa. Romulus killed his brother in a dispute over the location of their new city and became the first king of Rome.

Rome's early history is marked by its interaction with its neighbours, especially the Etruscans, who ruled over most of central Italy. Rome gradually expanded its territory by conquering and assimilating other peoples, such as the Latins, the Sabines, and the Volsci. Rome also fought against foreign invaders, such as the Gauls, who sacked the city in 390 BC.

In 509 BC, Rome abolished its monarchy and became a republic, governed by elected magistrates and a senate. The republic was characterized by a series of wars and conflicts, both internal and external. The most famous ones are the Punic Wars against Carthage, which lasted from 264 to 146 BC and resulted in Rome's domination of the Mediterranean; the civil wars between Julius Caesar and Pompey, which ended with Caesar's assassination in 44 BC; and the civil wars between Octavian (later Augustus) and Mark Antony, which culminated in the Battle of Actium in 31 BC.

Augustus became the first emperor of Rome in 27 BC, ushering in a period of peace and prosperity known as the Pax Romana. The Roman Empire reached its peak under Trajan in the 2nd century AD when it controlled most of Europe, North Africa, and parts of Asia. The empire was divided into two halves by Diocletian in 284 AD and later reunited by Constantine in 324 AD. Constantine also moved the capital from Rome to Byzantium (later Constantinople) in 330 AD and legalized Christianity as a religion in 313 AD.

The decline of the Roman Empire is usually dated from the sack of Rome by the Visigoths in 410 AD. The western half of the empire collapsed in 476 AD when the last emperor was deposed by a Germanic chief. The eastern half, known as the Byzantine Empire, survived until 1453 AD. Rome itself became part of various kingdoms and states, such as the Ostrogothic Kingdom, the Lombard Kingdom, the Papal States, and the Kingdom of Italy.

Rome's history is not only ancient, but also medieval, Renaissance, Baroque, modern, and contemporary. Throughout its long existence, Rome has been a centre of culture, religion, politics, and art. It has influenced and been influenced by countless civilizations and peoples. It has witnessed glory and tragedy, beauty and horror, innovation and decay. It is a city that deserves to be explored and admired by travellers from all over the world.

Why Visit Rome?

There are many reasons to visit this amazing city, but below are some of the most compelling ones:

Rome is a city of history. You can walk in the footsteps of emperors, gladiators, popes, and artists, and see the monuments and buildings that they left behind. You can marvel at the Colosseum, the Roman Forum, the Pantheon, and the Palatine Hill, where the ancient Romans lived and ruled. You can also explore the catacombs, the aqueducts, and the Appian Way, where the early Christians were buried and martyred.

Rome is a city of culture. You can admire some of the most famous artworks in the world, such as the Sistine Chapel, the Pietà, and the Laocoön. You can also visit some of the most renowned museums and galleries, such as the Vatican Museums, the Capitoline Museums, and the Borghese Gallery. You can also enjoy the opera, the theatre, and the cinema, as Rome is a hub of artistic expression and creativity.

Rome is a city of religion. You can experience the spiritual and sacred atmosphere of Vatican City, where you can see St. Peter's Basilica, the largest church in the world, and St. Peter's Square, where you can witness the Pope's blessings and audiences. You can also visit some of the most beautiful and historic churches in Rome, such as Santa Maria Maggiore, San Giovanni in Laterano, and Santa Maria in Trastevere. You can also join the pilgrims who flock to Rome for special occasions, such as Easter and Christmas.

Rome is a city of food and wine. You can taste some of the most delicious and authentic dishes in Rome, such as carbonara, amatriciana, cacio e pepe, and saltimbocca. You can also sample some of the best pizza, gelato, coffee, and pastries that Rome has to offer. You can also enjoy some of the finest wines from Italy and beyond, as Rome has a long tradition of wine-making and drinking.

Rome is a city of beauty. You can be enchanted by the stunning views and landscapes that Rome has to offer, such as the Tiber River, the Seven Hills, and the

Castel Sant'Angelo. You can also admire the elegant architecture and design that adorn Rome's streets and squares, such as the Trevi Fountain, the Spanish Steps, and Piazza Navona. You can also discover some of the hidden gems and secrets that Rome has to offer, such as the Aventine Keyhole, the Mouth of Truth, and the Capuchin Crypt.

Rome is a city that will make you fall in love with its culture, history, art, and people. It is a city that will inspire you to learn more about its past, present, and future. It is a city that you will never forget. It is a city that you should visit at least once in your lifetime.

Chapter 2 • Planning Your Trip

Best Time to Visit Rome

Rome is a city that can be enjoyed in any season, but some months are better than others depending on what you are looking for. Below are some factors to consider when choosing when to visit Rome:

Weather: Rome has a Mediterranean climate, which means mild winters and hot summers. The average temperature in January is 8°C (46°F), while in July it is 25°C (77°F). However, the weather can vary depending on the season and the location. For example, the hills around Rome can be cooler and wetter than the city centre, while the coast can be warmer and breezier. Generally, the best months for pleasant weather are April, May, September, and October, when the days are sunny and the nights are cool. The worst months are July and August, when the heat and humidity can be unbearable, especially in crowded places.

Crowds: Rome is a popular tourist destination all year round, but some periods are busier than others. The peak season is from June to August when schools are closed and many people take their summer vacations. This means long lines, higher prices, and limited availability for hotels and attractions. The low season is from November to February when fewer tourists visit Rome and the city is quieter and cheaper. However, some attractions may have shorter opening hours or be closed for maintenance. The shoulder season is from March to May and from September to October when the crowds are moderate and the weather is mild. This is considered by many travellers as the best time to visit Rome, as you can enjoy the city without too much hassle or expense.

Events: Rome hosts many events throughout the year that can enhance your experience or make it more challenging. Some of the most important ones are related to religion, such as Easter, Christmas, and the Pope's blessings and audiences. These events attract millions of pilgrims who come to see the Vatican City and its stunning attractions, such as St. Peter's Basilica and the Vatican Museums. If you want to witness these events, you should book your accommodation and tickets well in advance. Other events are related to culture, such as festivals, concerts, shows, and exhibitions that showcase the artistic and creative side of Rome. Some of these events are seasonal, such as Cosmophonies (June-July), Rock in Roma (July), and White Night of Rome (September), while others are annual, such as the International Horse Show (May), the International Literature Festival (May-June), and the Rome Marathon (April). If you want to attend these events, you should check their dates and locations before planning your trip.

In conclusion, the best time to visit Rome depends on your personal preferences and expectations. However, if you want to avoid extreme weather conditions and excessive crowds, you should aim for the shoulder seasons of spring and fall. If you don't mind the cold or the heat, you can find great deals and fewer tourists in winter or summer. If you want to experience some of the most famous events in Rome, you should plan and book early. Whatever time you choose, you will find a city full of charm, beauty, and wonder.

Visa Requirements and Travel Documents

Rome is the capital of Italy, which is a member of the European Union (EU) and the Schengen Area. This means that the same rules apply to Rome as to other EU and Schengen countries.

Depending on your country of origin, you may or may not need a visa to enter Rome for a short stay (up to 90 days). You will also need a valid passport and other supporting documents to prove your identity, travel arrangements, and financial means.

Below are some general guidelines on the visa requirements and travel documents for Rome:

If you are a citizen of an EU, EEA, or Schengen country, you do not need a visa to enter Rome. You only need a valid passport or national ID card. You can stay in Rome and other Schengen countries for up to 90 days within 180 days without any restrictions.

If you are a citizen of a non-EU, non-EEA, or non-Schengen country that has a visa exemption agreement with the Schengen Area, you do not need a visa to enter Rome either. You only need a valid passport with at least three months of validity beyond your intended departure date. You can also stay in Rome and other Schengen countries for up to 90 days within 180 days, but you may be asked to show proof of your travel itinerary, health insurance, and sufficient funds. Some of these countries are the USA, Canada, Australia, New Zealand, Japan, South Korea, Israel, Brazil, Argentina, Chile, Colombia, Mexico, etc.

If you are a citizen of a non-EU, non-EEA, or non-Schengen country that does not have a visa exemption agreement with the Schengen Area, you will need a visa to enter Rome. You will have to apply for a Schengen short-stay visa (also known as a C-type visa) at the Italian embassy or consulate in your country of residence. You will need to submit your passport with at least three months of validity beyond your intended departure date, two passport-sized photos, a completed application form, and other supporting documents depending on your purpose of travel. Some of these documents are proof of accommodation, round-trip ticket reservation, health insurance, invitation letter or sponsorship letter (if applicable), etc. You will also have to pay a visa fee and wait for the processing time, which may vary from one country to another. Some of these countries are China, India, Russia, Turkey, Nigeria, South Africa, etc.

Please note that these are general guidelines and may not cover all the specific cases and scenarios. For more detailed and updated information on the visa requirements and travel documents for Rome, we recommend visiting the official website of the Ministry of Foreign Affairs of Italy or contacting the Italian embassy or consulate in your country of residence. We hope this information helps you prepare for your trip to Rome and enjoy its wonderful attractions.

Airports and Airlines

Rome is a major destination for travellers from all over the world, and it is well connected by air with many cities and countries. Rome has two airports: **Fiumicino (FCO)** and **Ciampino (CIA)**. Depending on your origin, budget, and preference, you may fly to either of them.

Fiumicino Airport, also known as Leonardo da Vinci Airport, is the main international airport of Rome. It is located about 40 kilometres (25 miles) southwest of the city centre, on the coast of the Tyrrhenian Sea. Fiumicino Airport has four terminals: T1, T2, T3, and

T5. T1 and T2 are mainly used for domestic and Schengen flights, while T3 and T5 are used for international and intercontinental flights.

Fiumicino Airport is served by many airlines, including the national carrier Alitalia, as well as other major airlines such as Air France, British Airways, Lufthansa, American Airlines, Delta, United, Emirates, Qatar Airways, and more. Fiumicino Airport also offers direct flights to Rome from several U.S. cities, such as Atlanta, Boston, Charlotte, Chicago, Dallas, Los Angeles, Miami, New York, Philadelphia, and Washington.

Ciampino Airport, also known as G.B. Pastine Airport, is the secondary airport of Rome. It is located about 12.5 kilometres (7.5 miles) southeast of the city centre. Ciampino Airport has only one terminal that handles both arrivals and departures.

Ciampino Airport is mainly used by low-cost and charter airlines, such as Ryanair, Wizz Air, easyJet, Vueling, Blue Air, and more. Ciampino Airport offers flights to Rome from many European destinations, especially in the UK, Ireland, Spain, France, Germany, Poland, Romania, and more.

Both airports have facilities and services for travellers, such as shops, restaurants, bars, ATMs, currency exchange offices, car rental desks, information desks, and luggage storage lockers. Both airports also offer various options for transportation to and from the city centre, such as:

Taxi: The official taxi fare from Fiumicino Airport to central Rome is 48 euros (fixed rate), while from Ciampino Airport it is 30 euros (fixed rate). The taxi ride takes about 30-45 minutes depending on traffic.

Train: The Leonardo Express train connects Fiumicino Airport with Termini Station (the main train station in Rome) in about 30 minutes. The ticket costs 14 euros one way. The FL4 regional train connects Ciampino Airport with Termini Station in about 15 minutes. The ticket costs 1.50 euros one way.

Bus: Several bus companies operate between the airports and the city centre or other locations in Rome. The bus ride takes about 40-60 minutes depending on traffic. The ticket costs between 4-7 euros one way.

When planning your trip to Rome by air, you should consider several factors such as the availability of flights from your origin or destination; the cost of tickets; the distance and convenience of transportation between the airport and the city centre; the facilities and services at the airport; and your personal preference. You can use online tools such as Skyscanner to compare flights and prices from different airlines and airports.

Rome awaits you with its amazing attractions and experiences. Whether you fly to Fiumicino or Ciampino airport, you will find a way to reach the heart of Rome and enjoy its wonders. Buon viaggio!

Currency and Money Matters

Below are some tips and information to help you manage your budget and expenses in Rome.

The currency in Rome is the euro (EUR), which is the official currency of Italy and most of the European Union. One euro is divided into 100 cents, and you will see the symbol € used to show prices. You can find euro banknotes in denominations of 5, 10, 20, 50, 100, 200, and 500, but the 200 and 500 notes are rarely used. You can also find euro coins in denominations of 1 and 2 euros, and cents in denominations of 1, 2, 5, 10, 20, and 50.

The exchange rate between the euro and other currencies may vary depending on the market conditions and the service provider. You can use an online currency converter to check the current exchange rate before your trip. You can also use the Wise debit card to spend in euros without rip-off fees or hidden charges.

You can exchange your currency for euros at various places in Rome, such as banks, post offices, exchange bureaus, or hotels. However, you should be aware that some of these places may charge high commissions or offer unfavourable rates. You should always compare the exchange rate with the mid-market rate (the true exchange rate) and ask about any fees before exchanging your money.

You can also withdraw euros from ATMs (called Bancomat in Italy) using your debit or credit card. You can find ATMs easily in Rome, especially in the city centre and near tourist attractions. However, you should check with your bank about any fees or limits for using your card abroad. You should also always choose to be charged in euros when withdrawing from ATMs, as choosing your currency may result in a higher conversion rate.

You can pay by credit or debit card in most places in Rome, especially in hotels, restaurants, shops, and museums. However, some smaller or rural places may not accept cards or may charge extra fees for card payments. You should always carry some cash with you for emergencies or small purchases. You should also inform your bank about your travel plans to avoid any problems with your card transactions.

You can save money on your trip to Rome by following some simple tips, such as:

Avoiding peak season (June-August) and high-demand periods (Easter, Christmas, etc.), when prices are higher and crowds are larger.

Booking your accommodation and tickets in advance to get better deals and avoid queues.

Using public transportation or walking instead of taxis or private cars.
Eating at local or street food places instead of touristy or expensive restaurants.

Visiting free or discounted attractions, such as churches, parks, fountains, or museums on certain days or hours.

Getting a city pass or a travel card that gives you access to multiple attractions and transportation options for a fixed price.

Transportation in Rome

Rome has a public transportation system that consists of buses, trams, metro, and suburban trains that connect different parts of the city and its surroundings. However, the system is not very extensive, reliable, or user-friendly compared to other European cities. Therefore, you should also consider other options such as walking, cycling, or taking a taxi. Below are some tips and information to help you get around Rome:

Metro: The metro is the fastest and most convenient way to travel in Rome, especially if you want to reach the main tourist attractions such as the Vatican, the Colosseum, or the Spanish Steps. The metro has three lines: A (orange/red), B (blue), and C (green). The A and B lines intersect at Termini Station, the main train station in Rome. The C line is still under construction and has not reached the city centre yet. The metro runs from 5:30 a.m. to 11:30 p.m. every day, except on Fridays and Saturdays when it runs until 1:30 a.m. The ticket costs 1.50 euros and is valid for 100 minutes on any public transport in Rome. You can also buy a 24-hour ticket for 7 euros, a 48-hour ticket for 12.50 euros, or a 72-hour ticket for 18 euros. You can buy tickets at the ticket machines or booths at the metro stations, or newsagents or kiosks near the stations.

Bus: The bus is the most widespread and frequent means of public transportation in Rome, with over 300 lines and 8000 stops. The bus can take you to places that the metro does not cover, such as Trastevere, Villa Borghese, or Piazza Navona. However, the bus can also be slow, crowded, and unpredictable due to traffic jams, strikes, or breakdowns. The bus runs from 5:30 a.m. to midnight every day, but some night buses run until 5:30 a.m. The ticket costs 1.50 euros and is valid for 100 minutes on any public transport in Rome. You can also buy a 24-hour ticket for 7 euros, a 48-hour ticket for 12.50 euros, or a 72-hour ticket for 18 euros. You can buy tickets at the ticket machines or booths at some bus stops, or newsagents or kiosks near the stops. You must validate your ticket on board the bus by inserting it into the yellow machine.

Tram: The tram is another option for public transportation in Rome, but it is not very common or useful for tourists. There are only six tram lines and they do not reach the city centre or the main attractions. The tram runs from 5:30 a.m. to midnight every day. The ticket costs 1.50 euros and is valid for 100 minutes on any public transport in Rome. You can also buy a 24-hour ticket for 7 euros, a 48-hour ticket for 12.50 euros, or a 72-hour ticket for 18 euros. You can buy tickets at the ticket machines or booths at some tram stops, or newsagents or kiosks near the stops. You must validate your ticket on board the tram by inserting it into the yellow machine.

Suburban Train: The suburban train is another option for public transportation in Rome, but it is mainly used by commuters or travellers who want to reach destinations outside of Rome, such as Civitavecchia (the cruise port), Ostia (the beach), or Tivoli (the villa). There are three suburban train lines: FL1, FL3, and FL5. They connect with the metro at some stations such as Tiburtina (FL1), Valle Aurelia (FL3), and Ostiense (FL5). The suburban train runs from early morning until late night every day. The ticket price depends on the distance and destination of your trip.

You can buy tickets at the ticket machines or booths at the train stations. You must validate your ticket before boarding the train by inserting it into the green machine.

Taxi: Taxi is another option for transportation in Rome, but it is not very cheap or reliable. There are many taxis in Rome, but they are not always easy to find or hail on the street. You can either call a taxi company by phone or use an app such as Free Now or It Taxi. You can also find taxi stands at some locations such as Termini Station, Piazza Venezia, or Piazza di Spagna. The taxi fare is calculated by a meter that starts at 3 euros and increases by 1.10 euros per kilometre during the day and 1.30 euros per kilometre at night. There are also some extra charges for luggage, airport transfers, or holidays. The official taxi fare from Fiumicino Airport to central Rome is 48 euros (fixed rate), while from Ciampino Airport it is 30 euros (fixed rate). The taxi ride takes about 30-45 minutes depending on traffic.

Walking: Walking is one of the best ways to explore Rome, as the city is very walkable and full of sights and attractions. You can discover the beauty of Rome by strolling through its streets and squares, admiring its monuments and fountains, and enjoying its atmosphere and charm. Walking is also free, healthy, and environmentally friendly. However, you should also be careful of the traffic, the cobblestones, and the pickpockets when walking in Rome.

Cycling: Cycling is another option for transportation in Rome, but it is not very popular or safe. There are not many bike lanes or paths in Rome, and the traffic can be chaotic and dangerous for cyclists. However, there are some areas where cycling can be enjoyable and convenient, such as along the Tiber River, in the Villa Borghese Park, or the Appia Antica park. You can rent a bike from some shops or stations in Rome, or use a bike-sharing service such as Mobike or Jump. The rental price varies depending on the provider and the duration of your ride.

Accommodation Options

Below are some tips and information to help you choose the best accommodation option for your trip to Rome:

Hotels: Hotels are the most common and convenient option for accommodation in Rome, as they provide comfort, service, and facilities for their guests. You can find hotels of different categories and prices in Rome, from 5-star hotels that offer elegance and sophistication, to 2-star hotels that offer basic and affordable rooms. You can also find hotels of different styles and themes, such as boutique hotels, design hotels, historic hotels, or family-friendly hotels. Some of the best hotels in Rome are Hotel Maalot, J. K. Place Roma, Rocco Forte House, W Rome, and The St. Regis Rome.

Bed and Breakfasts: Bed and breakfasts are another option for accommodation in Rome, especially if you are looking for a more personal and intimate experience. Bed and breakfasts are usually small and family-run establishments that offer rooms with private or shared bathrooms, and breakfast is included in the price. You can find bed and breakfasts in different locations and neighbourhoods in Rome, from the historic centre to the outskirts. Some of the best bed and breakfasts in Rome are Relais Donna Lucrezia, La Maison D'Art Spagna, Residenza Monfy, The Fifteen Keys Hotel, and Relais Le Clarisse.

Apartments: Apartments are another option for accommodation in Rome, especially if you are looking for more space, privacy, and flexibility. Apartments are self-catering units that offer one or more bedrooms, a living room, a kitchen, and a bathroom. You can find apartments of different sizes and prices in Rome, from studio apartments to penthouses. You can also find apartments of different styles and features, such as modern apartments, rustic apartments, or apartments with balconies or terraces. Some of the best apartments in Rome are Navona Penthouse Suite & Terrace, Colosseum Corner Apartment, Domus Spagna Capo le Case Prestige Suite, Piazza di Spagna View Apartment, and Vatican Luxury Suites & Terrace.

Hostels: Hostels are another option for accommodation in Rome, especially if you are looking for a cheap and social experience. Hostels are shared dormitories that offer beds with lockers, shared bathrooms, and common areas. You can find hostels of different types and prices in Rome, from youth hostels to boutique hostels. You can also find hostels of different atmospheres and activities, such as party hostels, quiet hostels, or hostels with free tours or events. Some of the best hostels in Rome are The Yellow Hostel, Generator Rome Hostel, Alessandro Palace & Bar Hostel, Roma Scout Center Hostel, and The Beehive Hostel & Hotel.

Chapter 3 • Roman Culture and Etiquette

Roman Language and Basic Phrases

Rome is a city that has a diverse linguistic heritage, influenced by its history and geography. The official language of Rome is Italian, which is the national language of Italy and one of the most widely spoken languages in the world. However, Rome also has its dialect, known as Romanesco, which is spoken by many locals and reflects the unique identity and humour of the Roman people.

Romanesco is a variant of Italian that has some differences in vocabulary, grammar, pronunciation, and intonation. Romanesco originated from the Vulgar Latin that was spoken in ancient Rome and evolved with the influence of other languages, such as Greek, Germanic, French, Spanish, and Arabic. Romanesco also incorporates many slang words and expressions that are typical of the Roman way of life.

Romanesco is not a standardized or official language, but rather a colloquial and informal way of speaking that varies from person to person and from neighbourhood to neighbourhood. Romanesco is mostly used in casual and familiar situations, such as among friends, family, or strangers on the street. Romanesco is not usually taught in schools or used in formal or professional settings, where standard Italian is preferred.

However, Romanesco is not only a dialect but also a cultural and artistic expression of Rome. Romanesco has been used by many famous writers, poets, actors, and singers who have contributed to the literary and musical heritage of Rome. Some examples are Giuseppe Gioachino Belli, Trilussa, Aldo Fabrizi, Alberto Sordi, Nino Manfredi, Gigi Proietti, Antonello Venditti, Claudio Baglioni, and Francesco De Gregori.

If you want to learn some basic phrases in Romanesco to impress the locals or to understand their jokes and references, below are some examples:

Aò! - Hello
Come te butta? - How's it going?
Avoja! - Sure!
Ammazza! - Wow!

Daje! - Come on!

Da paura! - Awesome!

Scialla - Calm

Anvedi! - Check it out!

Che schifo! - How disgusting!

Che palle! - What a drag!

Me cojoni! - You're kidding me!

Coatto - Rude

Er mejo - The best

Er più - The most

Mannaggia - Darn

Mo' - Now

Nun ce posso crede - I can't believe it

Pe' fa' prima - To make it short

Quanno ce vo' ce vo' - When it's needed it's needed

Semo tutti romani - We're All Romans

These are just some of the many words and phrases that you can hear and use in Rome. However, you should also remember that Romanesco is not a fixed or universal language, but rather a dynamic and creative one that changes according to the context and the speaker. Therefore, you should always pay attention to the tone and the gestures of the person who is speaking to understand their meaning and intention.

By learning some basic phrases in Romanesco, you can communicate with the locals and appreciate their culture and humour. Buon viaggio!

Cultural Norms and Customs

Below are some tips and information to help you understand and respect the Roman culture and customs:

Greetings: Romans are friendly and warm people who like to greet each other with a smile and a handshake. When meeting someone for the first time, you should use formal titles such as Signore (Mr.), Signora (Mrs.), or Signorina (Miss), followed by their surname. When meeting someone you know well, you can use their first name or a nickname, and greet them with a kiss on each cheek. You should also say Buongiorno (Good morning) or Buonasera (Good evening) depending on the time of day.

Dress code: Romans are fashion-conscious and like to dress well and elegantly. You should avoid wearing casual or sloppy clothes, especially in the city centre or in formal settings. You should also dress modestly when visiting churches or religious sites, as you may be denied entry if you wear shorts, skirts, tank tops, or hats. You should also remove your sunglasses when talking to someone, as it is considered rude to hide your eyes.

Dining etiquette: Romans love food and wine, and dining is an important part of their culture and social life. When dining in Rome, you should follow some basic rules of etiquette, such as:

Wait for the host or the waiter to show you your seat, and do not start eating until everyone is served.

Use your fork in your left hand and your knife in your right hand, and do not switch them.

Do not cut your pasta with a knife or a fork, but twirl it with your fork on a spoon.

Do not ask for cheese on seafood dishes, as it is considered a culinary sin.

Do not ask for tap water, but order bottled water (still or sparkling) instead.

Do not ask for coffee during or after a meal, but order espresso or cappuccino after dessert.

Do not tip more than 10% of the bill, as service is usually included.

Gestures: Romans are expressive and communicative people who like to use gestures to emphasize their words or emotions. Some of the most common gestures are:

The OK sign: This gesture is made by forming a circle with the thumb and index finger, and it means OK or good.

The chin flick: This gesture is made by flicking the fingers under the chin, and it means I don't care or get lost.

The cheek screw: This gesture is made by twisting the index finger on the cheek, and it means delicious or good-looking.

The horn sign: This gesture is made by extending the index and little finger while curling the middle and ring finger, and it means watch out or cuckold.

Dining Etiquette

When dining in Rome, you should follow some basic rules of etiquette, such as:

Reservations: Romans usually dine late, around 8 or 9 p.m., and restaurants can be very busy and crowded during peak hours. Therefore, it is advisable to make a reservation in advance, especially for popular or high-end restaurants. You can call the restaurant directly or use online platforms such as The Fork or OpenTable to book your table.

Greetings: When you arrive at the restaurant, you should greet the staff with a smile and a Buonasera (Good evening). You should wait for the host or the waiter to show you your seat, and do not start eating until everyone is served. You should also say Grazie (Thank you) when the staff brings you your food or drinks, and Buon appetito (Enjoy your meal) to your companions before eating.

Ordering: When ordering your food and drinks, you should follow the typical structure of an Italian meal, which consists of antipasti (appetizers), primi (pasta or soup), secondi (meat or fish), contorni (side dishes), and dolci (dessert). You can also order pizza, which is usually eaten as a main course on its own. You are not obliged to order every course, but you should order at least one main course. You should also order your wine only after you have chosen your food, as the wine should match the dish. You can ask the waiter for recommendations or suggestions if you are unsure.

Eating: When eating your food, you should use your fork in your left hand and your knife in your right hand, and do not switch them. You should also avoid cutting your pasta with a knife or a fork, but twirl it with your fork on a spoon. You should also avoid asking for cheese on seafood dishes, as it is considered a culinary sin. You should eat everything on your plate, as leaving food is considered rude and wasteful.

Drinking: When drinking your wine or water, you should always toast with your companions before taking a sip. You should say Salute (Cheers) and look into the eyes of the person you are toasting with. You should also never fill your glass, but wait for someone else to do it for you. You should also avoid drinking too much alcohol, as being drunk is considered disrespectful and shameful.

Paying: When you finish your meal, you should ask for the bill by saying Il conto per favore (The bill please). You should pay the exact amount or round up to the nearest euro. You should not tip more than 10% of the bill, as service is usually included. However, if you are very satisfied with the service, you can leave some extra change on the table as a gesture of appreciation.

Leaving: When you leave the restaurant, you should say Arrivederci (Goodbye) and Grazie mille (Thank you very much) to the staff. You should also compliment the food and the service by saying Complimenti (Compliments) or Tutto buonissimo (Everything was delicious). You should also leave a positive review online if you enjoyed your experience.

Dress Code and Fashion in Rome

Below are some tips and information to help you dress like a local in Rome:

The general dress code in Rome is smart casual, which means wearing clothes that are neat, clean, and well-fitted, but not too formal or flashy. For women, skirts, dresses, and elegant trousers are in vogue; for men, stylish pants and polo shirts are all the rage. If you opt for jeans, that's okay; just ensure that they don't have rips or holes in them. And when evening hits and the temperatures dip, Romans never reach for a hoodie or chunky cardigan.

The colours and patterns that you choose for your clothes can also make a difference in your appearance. Romans tend to favour neutral colours such as black, white, beige, and navy, as well as jewel tones such as burgundy, emerald, and sapphire. These colours are easy to mix and match, and they also look classy and refined. Patterns such as stripes, checks, and florals are also popular, but avoid anything too loud or flashy.

The accessories that you wear can also enhance your outfit and show your personality. Romans love to accessorize with scarves, hats, sunglasses, jewellery, belts, and bags. However, you should avoid wearing too many or too large accessories at once, as they can look overwhelming or tacky. Instead, choose one or two statement pieces that complement your clothes and your style.

The shoes that you wear are also important for your comfort and your fashion sense. Romans are fashion-conscious and like to wear shoes that are stylish and elegant, such as heels, flats, loafers, or boots. However, they are also practical and know that walking on the cobblestone streets of Rome can be challenging and tiring. Therefore, they choose shoes that are comfortable and durable, as well as chic. You should avoid wearing sneakers or flip-flops in Rome unless you are going to the gym or the beach.

The dress code for religious sites in Rome is more strict than the general dress code. When visiting churches or other sacred places such as the Vatican or the Colosseum, you should dress modestly and respectfully. This means covering your shoulders and knees with clothes that are not too tight or revealing. You should also remove your hat or sunglasses when entering a church. You can bring a scarf or a cardigan with you to cover up if needed.

Festivals and Celebrations

Rome celebrates its culture and traditions with many festivals and events throughout the year. Some of these festivals are religious, some are artistic, some are historical, and some are just fun and festive. Below are some of the most popular and interesting festivals and celebrations that you can enjoy in Rome:

Natale di Roma: This festival commemorates the legendary founding of Rome by Romulus on April 21, 753 BC. Every year on this date, Rome hosts a series of festivities and events, such as concerts, parades, historical reenactments, fireworks, and gladiator shows. The main attractions are the Circo Massimo, where you can see ancient Roman games and races, and the

Campidoglio, where you can see the mayor of Rome cut a giant birthday cake for the city.

Festa della Repubblica: This festival celebrates the birth of the Italian Republic on June 2, 1946, when Italians voted to abolish the monarchy and establish a democratic government. Every year on this date, Rome hosts a grand military parade along Via dei Fori Imperiali, where you can see the president of Italy, the prime minister, and other dignitaries. The parade is followed by an air show by the Italian Air Force over the Colosseum. You can also visit the Quirinale Palace, the official residence of the president, which is open to the public on this day.

Estate Romana: This festival is also known as the Roman Summer Festival, and it lasts from June to September. It is a cultural extravaganza that features hundreds of events and activities in various locations around the city. You can enjoy outdoor cinema on Isola Tiberina, live music and theatre in Villa Ada or Villa Celimontana, opera and ballet in the Baths of Caracalla, art exhibitions in museums and galleries, food and wine festivals along the Tiber River, and much more.

Sagra dell'Uva: This festival is also known as the Marino Wine Festival or the Festival of the Grape, and it takes place in October in Marino, a town near Rome. It is one of the oldest and most famous wine festivals in Italy, dating back to 1925. It celebrates the harvest of grapes and the production of wine with a week-long program of events, such as concerts, contests, markets, and tastings. The highlight of the festival is when a fountain in Marino's main square starts to flow with free wine instead of water for an hour.

Carnevale di Roma: This festival is also known as the Carnival of Rome or Mardi Gras, and it takes place in February or March before Lent. It is a colourful and lively celebration that features costumes, masks, floats, music, dancing, and parties. The main events are held in Piazza del Popolo, Piazza Navona, Piazza di Spagna, and Via del Corso. You can also see horse races along Via del Corso or puppet shows in Piazza Navona. The festival ends with a fireworks display over Castel Sant'Angelo.

Chapter 4 • Exploring Roman Neighbourhood

Centro Storico

Centro Storico is the historical centre of Rome, where you can admire the ancient monuments, Renaissance palaces, and baroque fountains that make the Eternal City so enchanting. It is a UNESCO World Heritage Site, and it includes attractions such as the **Colosseum**, the **Roman Forum**, the **Vatican City,** and the **Piazza Navona.** Some of the best hotels in Centro Storico are:

Hotel Abruzzi: A beautifully renovated and tastefully decorated hotel in a perfect location for sightseeing on foot and finding nearby restaurants. It is located right in front of the Pantheon and offers a stunning view of the ancient temple.

Singer Palace Hotel: A luxurious hotel with elegant rooms, a rooftop terrace, and a gourmet restaurant. It is located near the Trevi Fountain and the Spanish Steps, and it attracts elite locals and noteworthy foreign guests.

Palazzo Navona: A modern hotel with stylish rooms, a rooftop bar, and a fitness centre. It is located near Piazza

Navona and Campo de' Fiori, two of Rome's most lively squares.

Some of the best restaurants in Centro Storico are:

Ditirambo: A cosy trattoria that serves stellar traditional fare in a rustic setting with attentive service and great prices. The menu is ample, even touting several vegetarian dishes, and everything is extremely flavorful and comforting.

Pierluigi: A refined restaurant that excels at fish and seafood, with prices to match its high calibre entrées and clientele. It lies in a lovely but unassuming piazza behind Campo de' Fiori and provides traditional white tablecloth service with extremely professional but friendly waiters.

Open Baladin: A casual pub that offers the best burgers in the centre of Rome and one of the largest selections of beer on draft. A collaboration between two Italian breweries, Baladin and Birra del Borgo, Open Baladin has over 40 rotating beers on tap and tantalizing burger options.

Trastevere

Trastevere is a charming and lively neighbourhood on the west bank of the Tiber River, where you can experience the authentic and bohemian side of Rome. It is a great place to explore the narrow cobblestone streets, the colourful buildings, and the vibrant nightlife. Some of the top attractions in Trastevere are:

Santa Maria in Trastevere: This is one of the oldest churches in Rome, dating back to the 4th century. It has a beautiful mosaic facade, a stunning 12th-century apse, and a golden ceiling.

Basilica of Santa Cecilia in Trastevere: This is another ancient church, dedicated to the patron saint of music. It has a 9th-century mosaic, a 13th-century fresco by Pietro Cavallini, and a crypt with the relics of Saint Cecilia.

Gianicolo Hill: This is a scenic spot that offers panoramic views of Rome and its monuments. It is also a historical site, where you can see a statue of Giuseppe Garibaldi, who fought for the unification of Italy, and a cannon that fires every day at noon.

Some of the best hotels in Trastevere are:

Horti 14 Borgo Trastevere: This is a modern and family-run hotel, located near the Botanic Gardens and the river. It has a garden terrace and bar, where you can relax and enjoy a drink. The rooms are spacious and comfortable, with a garden view.

Hotel Santa Maria: This is a cozy and charming hotel, located in a former convent from the 16th century. It has a courtyard with orange trees, where you can have breakfast or an aperitif. The rooms are simple and elegant, with wooden beams and terracotta floors.

Grand Hotel Gianicolo: This is a luxurious and refined hotel, located on the Gianicolo Hill. It has a pool and gardens, where you can admire the view of the Vatican and St. Peter's Basilica. The rooms are elegant and spacious, with marble bathrooms and balconies.

Some of the best restaurants in Trastevere are:

Da Enzo al 29: This is one of the best restaurants for traditional Roman food, such as carbonara, amatriciana, cacio e pepe, and artichokes. It is located near Santa Cecilia Basilica, and it has a rustic and cosy atmosphere.

La Cuverie: This is one of the best wine bars in Trastevere, where you can taste different wines from Italy and France, paired with cheese and charcuterie boards. It is located near Piazza Trilussa, and it has a modern and elegant decor.

Trapizzino: This is one of the best places for street food in Trastevere, where you can try trapizzino, a triangular pizza pocket filled with various toppings, such as meatballs, chicken cacciatore, or tripe. It is located near Piazza San Cosimato, and it has a casual and friendly vibe.

Monti

Monti is a trendy and historical neighbourhood near the Colosseum and the Roman Forum, where you can find hip cafes, vintage shops, and street art. Monti is a place where you can experience the modern and creative side of Rome, as well as its rich history and culture. Some of the top attractions in Monti are:

The Colosseum: This is the most iconic monument of Rome, a massive amphitheatre that hosted gladiator fights, animal hunts, and public executions in ancient times. You can visit the interior of the Colosseum and admire its impressive architecture and engineering.

Roman Forum: This is the heart of ancient Rome, where you can see the ruins of temples, basilicas, arches, and palaces that were once the centre of political, religious, and social life. You can walk along the Via Sacra, the main street of the Forum, and imagine what it looked like in its glory days.

Mercato Monti: This is a popular market that takes place every weekend in a former convent. You can find a variety of items, such as vintage clothing, accessories, books, art, and crafts. Mercato Monti is a great place to shop for unique souvenirs and support local artists and designers.

Some of the best hotels in Monti are:

Monti Palace Hotel: This is a designed hotel with a modern restaurant and bar. The elegant rooms offer a smart TV and free Wi-Fi. The hotel is located just 100 meters from Cavour Metro Station and a 10-minute walk from the Colosseum.

Rooms Roma - Monti: This is a stylish hotel with individually designed rooms and flat-screen TVs with satellite channels. The hotel is located a 5-minute walk from Rome Termini Train Station and offers free breakfast.

Salotto Monti: This is a chic boutique hotel with 12 rooms, decorated with sash windows, wood floors, and wallpaper by Fornasetti. The hotel has a breakfast terrace with wonderful views across the city.

Some of the best restaurants in Monti are:

La Taverna dei Fori Imperiali: This is a family-run restaurant that serves excellent traditional Roman food, such as carbonara, amatriciana, cacio e pepe, and artichokes. The restaurant is located near the Roman Forum and has a cosy and friendly atmosphere.

Al vino Al vino: This is one of the best wine bars in Monti, where you can taste different wines from Italy and abroad, paired with cheese and charcuterie boards. The bar is located near Piazza Madonna dei Monti and has a modern and elegant decor.

Gelateria dell'Angeletto: This is one of the best gelato shops in Monti, where you can try vegan gelato that tastes like biting into the best hazelnut you've ever had. The shop is located near Piazza degli Zingari and has a casual and friendly vibe.

Testaccio

Testaccio is a historical and lively neighbourhood south of the city centre, famous for its food market, nightlife, and street art. Testaccio is a place where you can taste traditional Roman dishes, such as tripe, carbonara, and pizza al taglio. It is also home to the Pyramid of Cestius, an ancient tomb built in the 1st century BC. Some of the best hotels in Testaccio are:

Hotel Santa Prisca: A beautifully renovated and tastefully decorated hotel in a perfect location for sightseeing on foot and finding nearby restaurants. It is located right in front of the Pantheon and offers a stunning view of the ancient temple.

Hotel Villa San Pio: A luxurious hotel with elegant rooms, a rooftop terrace, and a gourmet restaurant. It is located near the Trevi Fountain and the Spanish Steps, and it attracts elite locals and noteworthy foreign guests.

Palazzo Navona: A modern hotel with stylish rooms, a rooftop bar, and a fitness centre. It is located near Piazza Navona and Campo de' Fiori, two of Rome's most lively squares.

Some of the best restaurants in Testaccio are:

Da Felice: A cosy trattoria that serves stellar traditional fare in a rustic setting with attentive service and great prices. The menu is ample, even touting several vegetarian dishes, and everything is extremely flavorful and comforting.

Pizzeria da Remo: A popular pizzeria that serves Romana-style pizzas – thin and crispy, topped with molten hot mozzarella. The pizzas are made with fresh ingredients and baked in a wood-fired oven.

Trapizzino: A casual pub that offers the best street food in Testaccio, where you can try trapizzino, a triangular pizza pocket filled with various toppings, such as meatballs, chicken cacciatore, or tripe.

Chapter 5 • Roman Cuisine and Food Experiences

Introduction to Roman Cuisine

One of the delights of visiting Rome is exploring its rich and varied cuisine, which reflects the history and culture of the city and its surroundings. Roman cuisine is based on fresh, seasonal and simple ingredients, often enhanced by herbs, spices and cheese.

Roman cuisine has evolved over centuries, influenced by the different political and social changes that the city has witnessed. From ancient times, when Rome was a powerful empire that traded with many regions and peoples, to the Renaissance, when the popes patronized some of the finest chefs of the time, to the modern era when new ingredients and dishes have been introduced by immigrants and travellers, Roman cuisine has always been a reflection of its creativity.

Some of the most typical Roman dishes are based on pasta, which is usually made from durum wheat and cut into various shapes and sizes. The four pillars of Roman pasta are amatriciana, cacio e pepe, carbonara and gricia, each with its distinctive sauce and flavour. Amatriciana is a spicy tomato sauce with guanciale (cured pork cheek) and pecorino cheese; cacio e pepe is a creamy sauce of black pepper and pecorino cheese; carbonara is a rich sauce of eggs, cheese, guanciale and black pepper; and gricia is a simple sauce of guanciale and pecorino cheese. These pasta dishes are usually served with bucatini or spaghetti, but sometimes also with rigatoni or tonnarelli.

Another staple of Roman cuisine is meat, especially lamb and pork. Lamb is often cooked as abbacchio, a young milk-fed lamb that is roasted or stewed with herbs and garlic. Pork is used in various ways, from porchetta, a whole roasted pig stuffed with herbs and spices, to saltimbocca, thin slices of veal topped with prosciutto and sage. Pork is also the main ingredient of many cured meats, such as prosciutto, salami and mortadella. One of the most characteristic features of Roman cuisine is the use of the quinto quarto, or the fifth quarter, which refers to the offal or innards of the animals. These include tripe, liver, kidneys, brains and even testicles, which are cooked in various ways, often with tomato sauce or vinegar.

Roman cuisine also makes use of fresh vegetables and seafood from the nearby countryside and coast. Some of the most popular vegetables are artichokes, peas, fava beans and chicory, which are prepared in different ways depending on the season. Artichokes are especially famous in Rome, where they are cooked as carciofi alla romana (braised with garlic and mint) or carciofi alla giudia (deep-fried until crispy). Seafood is also abundant in Rome, especially clams, mussels, anchovies and sardines. These are often used to make pasta sauces or soups, such as spaghetti alle vongole (with clams) or zuppa di cozze (with mussels).

No meal in Rome is complete without dessert, which can range from pastries to gelato to chocolate. Some of the most common pastries are pasticcini, small individual cakes that come in various flavours and shapes. Gelato is the Italian version of ice cream, which is made with milk instead of cream and has a smoother texture. Rome has many gelaterias that offer a wide selection of flavours, from classic ones like chocolate and vanilla to more exotic ones like pistachio and hazelnut. Chocolate lovers will also find plenty of options in Rome, from handmade chocolates and candies to cakes and cookies.

Roman cuisine is a feast for the senses that will make you fall in love with the city even more. Whether you choose a traditional trattoria or a modern restaurant, you will be able to enjoy some of the best dishes that Rome has to offer. Buon appetite

Famous Roman Dishes

Below are some of the most famous Roman dishes that you should not miss when you visit the city:

Pizza al taglio: This is a type of pizza that is baked in large rectangular trays and cut into slices of different sizes and shapes. You can choose from a wide range of toppings, such as cheese, tomato, ham, mushrooms, vegetables and more. Pizza al taglio is a popular street food that you can find in many bakeries and pizzerias around the city.

Supplì: These are fried rice balls stuffed with cheese and sometimes meat or vegetables. They are crispy on the outside and gooey on the inside and are usually eaten as a snack or appetizer. Supplì is often served with tomato sauce or mayonnaise.

Coda alla vaccinara: This is a stew made with oxtail, celery, carrots, onions, tomatoes and herbs. It is cooked for several hours until the meat becomes tender and falls off the bone. Coda alla vaccinara is a hearty dish that is typically served with bread or polenta.

Saltimbocca alla romana: This is a dish of thin slices of veal topped with prosciutto and sage, and cooked in white wine and butter. The name saltimbocca means "jump in the mouth", which describes how delicious and easy to eat this dish is. Saltimbocca alla romana is usually accompanied by roasted potatoes or salad.

Carciofi alla romana: These are artichokes that are braised with garlic, mint, parsley and olive oil. They are cooked until they become soft and tender, and are served as a side dish or a main course. Carciofi alla romana is a speciality of Rome, especially in spring when artichokes are in season.

Maritozzi con la panna: These are sweet buns filled with whipped cream. They are soft and fluffy and are often eaten for breakfast or as a dessert. Maritozzi con la panna is a traditional treat that dates back to the Middle Ages when they were given as gifts to lovers on certain occasions.

Wine and Food Pairing

Wine and food pairing is an art that can enhance your enjoyment of both the wine and the food. Rome offers a variety of dishes and wines that can create harmonious or contrasting pairings, depending on your preference. Below are some general tips and examples of wine and food pairing in Rome:

Balance the weight and intensity of the wine and the food. For example, a light salad with a vinaigrette dressing would pair well with a light and crisp white wine, such as Frascati Superiore. A rich and hearty pasta dish with a meat sauce would pair well with a full-bodied and robust red wine, such as Cesanese di Affile.

Match the acidity and sweetness of the wine and the food. For example, a tomato-based dish, such as pizza or pasta al pomodoro, would pair well with a high-acidity wine, such as Sangiovese or Barbera. A sweet dessert, such as maritozzi con la panna, would pair well with sweet wine, such as Cannellino di Frascati.

Consider the sauce and the seasoning of the dish. For example, a creamy sauce, such as carbonara or Alfredo, would pair well with a rich and buttery white wine, such as Chardonnay or Pinot Gris. A spicy dish, such as arrabbiata or amatriciana, would pair well with a fruity and low-tannin red wine, such as Montepulciano or Merlot.

Experiment with different combinations and discover your own preferences. There is no one right answer to wine and food pairing, as different people have different tastes and preferences. The most important thing is to have fun and enjoy the experience of tasting different wines and foods together.

Some examples of typical Roman dishes and wines that you can try are:

Carciofi alla romana (braised artichokes with garlic and mint) with **Grechetto**, a white wine with floral and herbal aromas and flavours.

Saltimbocca alla romana (veal scallops with prosciutto and sage) with **Cesanese di Affile**, a red wine with cherry and blackberry notes and smooth tannins.

Coda alla vaccinara (oxtail stew with celery, carrots, onions, tomatoes and herbs) with **Nero d'Avola,** a red wine with dark fruit and spice flavours and firm tannins.

Tiramisu (a dessert made with ladyfingers soaked in coffee and layered with mascarpone cheese and cocoa) with **Cannellino di Frascati**, a sweet white wine with honey and apricot aromas and flavours.

Culinary Experiences and Cooking Classes

Below are some of the options that you can choose from:

3-in-1 Fettuccine, Ravioli and Tiramisu Cooking Class in Rome: This is a fun and interactive cooking class that will teach you how to make three Italian classics: fettuccine, ravioli and tiramisu. You will learn how to prepare the dough, the filling and the sauce for the pasta, and how to whip up a delicious tiramisu with mascarpone cheese and coffee. You will also enjoy a glass of wine and a certificate of completion at the end of the class.

Combo Pizza and Pasta Cooking Class: This is a comprehensive cooking class that will cover two of the most popular dishes in Italy: pizza and pasta. You will learn how to make pizza dough from scratch, how to choose and apply the toppings, and how to bake it in a wood-fired oven. You will also learn how to make fresh pasta with different shapes and sauces, such as tagliatelle with bolognese sauce or ravioli with ricotta cheese and spinach. You will then enjoy your creations with wine and dessert.

Pizza Class in Rome around Piazza Navona: This is a pizza-making class that will take place in a historical setting near Piazza Navona. You will learn how to make pizza al taglio, which is a type of pizza that is baked in large rectangular trays and cut into slices. You will choose from a wide range of toppings, such as cheese, tomato, ham, mushrooms, vegetables and more. You will also learn some tips and tricks on how to make the perfect pizza at home.

Pasta and Tiramisu Home Cooking Class: This is a home cooking class that will take place in a cosy apartment in the centre of Rome. You will learn how to make pasta from scratch with a rolling pin and a pasta cutter, and how to make two different sauces: amatriciana and cacio e pepe. You will also learn how to make tiramisu, one of the most famous Italian desserts. You will then enjoy your meal with wine and coffee in a friendly atmosphere.

Cook a Classic Italian Meal Inspired by a Roman Grandmother: This is a cooking class that will teach you how to cook a classic Italian meal inspired by a

Roman grandmother. You will learn how to make dishes such as carciofi alla romana (braised artichokes with garlic and mint), saltimbocca alla romana (veal scallops with prosciutto and sage), coda alla vaccinara (oxtail stew with celery, carrots, onions, tomatoes and herbs), and maritozzi con la panna (sweet buns filled with whipped cream). You will also learn some stories and anecdotes about Roman cuisine and culture.

Chef in a Day Cooking Classes in Rome: This is a professional cooking class that will teach you how to make a gourmet 6-course Italian meal. You will receive one-on-one instruction from a trained chef, who will guide you through every step of the preparation. You will learn how to make dishes such as gnocchi with pesto sauce, stuffed zucchini flowers, lamb chops with rosemary potatoes, tiramisu and more. You will also receive an apron, a recipe book and a certificate of attendance.

Pasta Making with Wine Tasting and Dinner in Frascati: This is a culinary experience that will combine pasta making with wine tasting and dinner in Frascati, a charming town near Rome famous for its wine production. You will visit a local winery, where you will learn about the history and methods of winemaking in Frascati. You will then taste four different wines paired with cheese, salami and bread. You will also learn how to make fresh pasta with different sauces, such as carbonara or arrabbiata. You will then enjoy your pasta with wine and dessert on a panoramic terrace overlooking Rome.

Homemade Gelato and Pizza Cooking Class with Wine: This is a cooking class that will teach you how to make two of the most loved Italian treats: gelato and pizza. You will learn how to make gelato from scratch using milk instead of cream, which gives it a smoother texture. You will also learn how to make pizza dough from scratch using natural yeast, which makes it lighter and easier to digest. You will then choose your favourite toppings and bake your pizza in a wood-fired oven. You will also enjoy wine and soft drinks during the class.

Best Restaurants and Cafes

Below are some of the best restaurants and cafes that you can try in Rome:

That's Amore Restaurant by Fabio Bongianni: This is a cosy and elegant restaurant near the Trevi

Fountain, where you can taste the authentic traditions of the Roman trattorias. The menu features fresh pasta made by hand daily, succulent main dishes, fresh sides, and delicious homemade desserts. The restaurant also offers a selection of wines from Italy and abroad. Some of the specialities include fettuccine with porcini mushrooms and truffle, lamb chops with rosemary potatoes, and tiramisu.

433 Restaurant: This is a creative and stylish restaurant in the heart of the famous "triangle of drinking" near Piazza Navona. The restaurant offers a fusion of Italian and international cuisine, with dishes that are inspired by the seasons and the market. The restaurant also has a wine cellar with over 300 labels from around the world. Some of the dishes include pumpkin soup with ginger and coconut milk, tagliatelle with lobster and cherry tomatoes, and chocolate cake with salted caramel.

Ad Hoc Ristorante (Piazza del Popolo): This is a refined and romantic restaurant near Piazza del Popolo, where you can enjoy a gourmet Italian meal. The restaurant specializes in truffles, which are used in various dishes and sauces. The restaurant also has an extensive wine list, with over 800 labels from Italy and abroad. Some of the dishes include truffle beef tartare, spaghetti with black truffle and pecorino cheese, and truffle tiramisu.

Bufalero: This is a casual and friendly restaurant near Campo de Fiori, where you can savour the best buffalo mozzarella from Campania. The restaurant offers a variety of dishes that feature this cheese, such as salads, sandwiches, pizzas, kinds of pasta, and desserts. The restaurant also serves other Italian specialities, such as porchetta, salami, and prosciutto. Some of the dishes include buffalo mozzarella with cherry tomatoes and basil, pizza with buffalo mozzarella and ham, and cheesecake with buffalo ricotta.

La Fata Ignorante - Rooftop Restaurant & Bar: This is a rooftop restaurant and bar near Termini Station, where you can enjoy a panoramic view of Rome while dining on seafood and Italian cuisine. The restaurant has a modern and elegant decor, with a terrace that overlooks the city skyline. The menu features fresh fish and seafood from the Mediterranean Sea, as well as meat and vegetarian dishes. Some of the dishes include tuna tartare with avocado and mango, risotto with shrimp and zucchini flowers, and beef cheek with mashed potatoes.

Pinsitaly Trevi: This is a fast food restaurant near the Trevi Fountain, where you can taste the best pizza al Taglio in Rome. Pizza al Taglio is a type of pizza that is baked in large rectangular trays and cut into slices of different sizes and shapes. You can choose from a wide range of toppings, such as cheese, tomato, ham, mushrooms, vegetables and more. The restaurant also serves rice croquettes, salads, drinks, and desserts.

Il Fantino: This is a traditional trattoria near the Vatican City, where you can enjoy typical Roman cuisine in a cosy and family-friendly atmosphere. The menu features dishes that are made with fresh ingredients and cooked according to the recipes of the Roman grandmother. The portions are generous and the prices are reasonable. Some of the dishes include spaghetti alla carbonara, cacio e pepe or amatriciana; veal scaloppine with lemon or marsala sauce; artichokes alla romana or alla giudia; tiramisu or panna cotta.

Quel Che C'e Laboratorio di Cucina: This is a laboratory of cuisine near Piazza Navona, where you can experience the creativity and passion of the chef. The menu changes daily according to the availability of seasonal products and the inspiration of the chef. The dishes are innovative and original, combining different flavours and textures. The restaurant also has a wine bar with a selection of wines from small producers. Some of the dishes include pumpkin gnocchi with gorgonzola sauce; rabbit ragu with pistachio pesto; tuna tataki with sesame seeds.

"DOC" Cruderia EnoBistrot: This is a cruderia (raw bar) and enobistrot (wine bistro) near Piazza Barberini, where you can taste the best carpaccio in Rome. Carpaccio is a dish of thinly sliced raw meat or fish, seasoned with olive oil, lemon, salt, pepper, and other ingredients. The restaurant offers a variety of carpaccio, such as beef, salmon, tuna, swordfish, octopus, and more. The restaurant also serves salads, cheeses, cold cuts, and desserts. The restaurant also has a wine list with over 100 labels from Italy and abroad.

Bono Bottega Nostrana - Piazza di Spagna: This is a sandwich shop near Piazza di Spagna, where you can taste the best porchetta in Rome. Porchetta is a whole roasted pig stuffed with herbs and spices, which is sliced and served in a bun or on a plate. The sandwich shop offers different types of porchetta, such as classic, spicy, cheese, truffle, and more. The sandwich shop also serves salads, drinks, and desserts.

Bars and Nightlife

Below are some of the best bars and nightlife options that you can explore in Rome:

Aperitivo: Aperitivo is the Italian version of happy hour, which usually starts around 6 p.m. and lasts until 9 p.m. It is a great way to unwind after a day of sightseeing and to sample some of the local delicacies and drinks. Aperitivo usually consists of a drink (such as wine, beer, or a spritz) and a buffet of snacks (such as cheese, salami, pizza, pasta, and salads). Some of the best places to enjoy aperitivo in Rome are Freni e Frizioni, a trendy bar in Trastevere with a large outdoor terrace; Salotto 42, a chic lounge near Piazza di Pietra with a library and a fireplace; and Etabli, an elegant wine bar near Piazza Navona with a cosy atmosphere.

Pubs and Bars: If you are looking for a more casual and lively night out, you can head to one of the many pubs and bars in Rome. You will find a variety of options, from Irish pubs to craft beer bars, from wine bars to cocktail bars. Some of the best pubs and bars in Rome are The Abbey Theatre, an Irish pub near Piazza

Navona with live music and sports; Bir & Fud, a craft beer bar in Trastevere with more than 30 taps and delicious pizzas; and The Jerry Thomas Project, a speakeasy bar near Campo de' Fiori with creative cocktails and a secret password.

Clubs and Discos: If you want to dance the night away, you can choose from one of the many clubs and discos in Rome. You will find a range of music genres, from pop to rock, from techno to hip hop, from salsa to reggaeton. Some of the best clubs and discos in Rome are Goa, a stylish club in Ostiense with international DJs and a large dance floor; Shari Vari Playhouse, a multi-level club near Piazza Venezia with different rooms and music styles; and Lanificio 159, an alternative club in Pietralata with live concerts and art exhibitions.

Rooftops and Summer Bars: If you want to enjoy the view of Rome while sipping on a drink, you can visit one of the many rooftops and summer bars in Rome. You will find some of the most stunning panoramas of the city, from the Colosseum to the Vatican, from the river to the hills. Some of the best rooftops and summer bars in Rome are Terrazza Borromini, a rooftop bar near Piazza Navona with a breathtaking view of the dome of

Sant'Agnese in Agone; La Fata Ignorante, a rooftop restaurant near Termini Station with seafood and Italian cuisine; and Lungo il Tevere, a summer festival along the river near Tiber Island with outdoor bars and restaurants.

Chapter 6 • Top Attractions

The Colosseum and the Roman Forum

The Colosseum and the Roman Forum are two of the most iconic and impressive monuments of ancient Rome. They are both located in the heart of the city and are part of the UNESCO World Heritage Site of the Historic Centre of Rome. Visiting these sites is a must for anyone who wants to learn more about the history, culture, and entertainment of the Roman Empire.

The Colosseum, also known as the Flavian Amphitheatre, is the largest amphitheatre ever built in ancient Rome. It was commissioned by Emperor Vespasian in A.D. 72, and inaugurated by his son Titus in A.D. 80 with 100 days of games, including gladiatorial combats, wild animal fights, and mock naval battles. The Colosseum could hold up to 50,000 spectators, who were seated according to their social status. The Colosseum was also an engineering marvel, with a complex system of vaults, arches, and columns that supported the structure. It also had a retractable canvas roof that could provide shade for the audience. The Colosseum was used for entertainment for about four centuries until it fell into decay and neglect. Today, it is one of the most visited tourist attractions in Rome, and a symbol of the city and its long history.

The Roman Forum, or Forum Romanum, was the political, religious, and commercial centre of ancient Rome. It was the site of many important buildings and monuments, such as temples, basilicas, arches, and statues. The Roman Forum was also the place where public speeches, trials, elections, and ceremonies took place. Some of the most famous events that happened in the Roman Forum were the funeral of Julius Caesar, the speeches of Cicero, and the triumphs of Augustus. The Roman Forum was also connected to other forums that were built by different emperors, such as the Forum of Caesar, the Forum of Augustus, and the Forum of Trajan. The Roman Forum was gradually abandoned and buried under rubble after the fall of the Roman Empire. It was rediscovered and excavated in the 18th and 19th centuries. Today, it is one of the most fascinating archaeological sites in Rome, where visitors can admire the ruins of ancient Rome and imagine its glory.

The Colosseum and the Roman Forum are open to visitors every day from 8:30 a.m. to one hour before sunset. The admission ticket includes both sites and is valid for two consecutive days. It is recommended to book online in advance to avoid long queues at the entrance. It is also advisable to wear comfortable shoes and bring water and sunscreen, as there is not much shade in these sites. The Colosseum and the Roman Forum are both accessible by metro (line B), bus (line 75), or tram (line 3). Alternatively, you can join a guided tour or an audio tour that will provide you with more information and insights about these sites.

The Vatican City and the Sistine Chapel

The Vatican City and the Sistine Chapel are two of the most important and impressive attractions in Rome, both for their religious and artistic significance. They are located within the Vatican City State, the smallest sovereign state in the world, which is ruled by the Pope and has its currency, postal service, and army. The Vatican City and the Sistine Chapel are part of the UNESCO World Heritage Site of the Historic Centre of Rome.

The Vatican City is the seat of the Catholic Church and the home of the Pope. It covers an area of about 44 hectares (110 acres) and contains some of the most famous buildings and monuments of Christianity, such as St. Peter's Basilica, St. Peter's Square, the Apostolic Palace, the Vatican Museums, and the Vatican Gardens. The Vatican City also hosts many cultural and artistic treasures, such as paintings, sculptures, mosaics, tapestries, and books. Some of the most renowned artists who worked in the Vatican City include Michelangelo, Raphael, Bernini, and Bramante.

The Sistine Chapel is one of the highlights of the Vatican Museums and one of the most famous chapels in the world. It was built between 1473 and 1481 by Pope

Sixtus IV, from whom it takes its name. It is used for religious ceremonies and functions, especially for the papal conclave, the process by which a new pope is elected. The Sistine Chapel is famous for its magnificent frescoes that cover the walls and the ceiling, depicting scenes from the Bible and the history of Christianity. The most important frescoes are those by Michelangelo on the ceiling and the west wall behind the altar. The ceiling frescoes depict nine scenes from the Book of Genesis, such as The Creation of Adam and The Last Judgment. The west wall fresco depicts The Last Judgment, showing Christ judging the souls of the dead.

The Vatican City and the Sistine Chapel are open to visitors every day except Sundays and holidays. The admission ticket includes both sites and is valid for one day. It is recommended to book online in advance to avoid long queues at the entrance. It is also advisable to wear modest clothing that covers your shoulders and knees, as these are sacred places. The Vatican City and the Sistine Chapel are both accessible by metro (line A), bus (line 64), or tram (line 19). Alternatively, you can join a guided tour or an audio tour that will provide you with more information and insights about these sites.

The Pantheon and the Trevi Fountain

The Pantheon and the Trevi Fountain are two of the most remarkable and beautiful attractions in Rome, both for their architectural and historical significance. They are located within walking distance of each other and are part of the UNESCO World Heritage Site of the Historic Centre of Rome.

The Pantheon is one of the best-preserved and most influential buildings of ancient Rome. It was built as a temple to all the gods by Emperor Hadrian in A.D. 118-125, on the site of an earlier temple by Agrippa in 27 B.C. The Pantheon is famous for its dome, which is the largest unreinforced concrete dome in the world, and has an oculus (a circular opening) at the top that lets in natural light. The Pantheon also contains the tombs of several important figures, such as Raphael, Victor Emmanuel II, and Umberto I.

The Trevi Fountain, built in the 1700s, is perhaps one of Rome's most iconic structures. Erected on the site of an ancient Roman water source, the fountain is made of the same material as the Colosseum (travertine stone). The Trevi Fountain serves as a modern marvel that links back to Rome's fabled past. The fountain depicts Neptune, the god of the sea, riding a chariot pulled by two sea horses, surrounded by other mythological figures and allegories. The fountain is also famous for its legend that if you throw a coin over your left shoulder into the water, you will return to Rome someday.

The Pantheon and the Trevi Fountain are open to visitors every day for free. However, they can get very crowded during peak hours, so it is advisable to visit them early in the morning or late in the evening. The Pantheon and the Trevi Fountain are both accessible by bus (lines 40, 64, or 85), or by foot from other nearby attractions, such as Piazza Navona or Piazza Venezia. Alternatively, you can join a guided tour or an audio tour that will provide you with more information and insights about these sites

The Spanish Steps and the Piazza Navona

The Spanish Steps and the Piazza Navona are two of the most charming and picturesque attractions in Rome, both for their architectural and historical significance.

They are located within walking distance of each other and are part of the UNESCO World Heritage Site of the Historic Centre of Rome.

The Spanish Steps are a grand staircase with 135 steps that connect the Piazza di Spagna at the bottom with the church of Trinità dei Monti at the top. They were built between 1723 and 1725 by the Italian architect Francesco de Sanctis, with the funds left by a French diplomat, Etienne Gueffier. The name of the steps comes from the Spanish Embassy to the Holy See, which was located on the square below. The steps have been a popular spot for tourists and locals alike, who enjoy sitting on them and admiring the view of the city. The steps are also famous for being featured in many movies and books, such as Roman Holiday and The Roman Spring of Mrs Stone.

The Piazza Navona is one of the most beautiful and lively squares in Rome, with its three magnificent fountains, its elegant palaces, and its street artists and performers. The square was built on the site of an ancient Roman stadium, where athletic competitions and chariot races were held. The name of the square comes from the Latin word "agones", meaning "games". The square was transformed into a Baroque masterpiece in the 17th century by Pope Innocent X, who commissioned some of the most renowned artists of the time, such as Bernini, Borromini, and Rainaldi. The main attraction of the square is the Fountain of the Four Rivers, designed by Bernini in 1651. The fountain represents four major rivers of the world: the Nile, the Ganges, the Danube, and the Rio de la Plata. The fountain is topped by an Egyptian obelisk that was brought to Rome by Emperor Domitian.

The Spanish Steps and the Piazza Navona are open to visitors every day for free. However, they can get very crowded during peak hours, so it is advisable to visit them early in the morning or late in the evening. The Spanish Steps and the Piazza Navona are both accessible by bus (lines 40, 62, or 492) or by foot from other nearby attractions, such as the Trevi Fountain or the Pantheon. Alternatively, you can join a guided tour or an audio tour that will provide you with more information and insights about these sites.

Chapter 7 •
Accommodation
Recommendations

Luxury Resort Recommendations

Below are some luxury resort recommendations in Rome:

Rome Cavalieri, A Waldorf Astoria Resort: This is a five-star resort located on a hilltop overlooking the city, with a panoramic view of the Vatican, the Colosseum, and the Roman Forum. The resort features 345 rooms and suites, decorated with antique furniture and artworks, including paintings by masters such as Tiepolo and Warhol. The resort also offers a spa, a fitness centre, three outdoor pools, an indoor pool, a tennis court, and a golf course. The resort has four restaurants and bars, including La Pergola, the only three-Michelin-starred restaurant in Rome.

Six Senses Rome: This is a new luxury resort that opened in 2023, located in a historical building near Piazza Navona. The resort has 95 rooms and suites, designed with a blend of contemporary and classic elements, using natural materials and colours. The resort also has a spa, a fitness centre, an indoor pool, and a rooftop terrace. The resort has two restaurants and bars, serving Italian and international cuisine, with an emphasis on sustainability and wellness.

InterContinental Rome Ambasciatori Palace: This is a four-star resort located on the prestigious Via Veneto, near the Spanish Steps and the Trevi Fountain. The resort has 152 rooms and suites, furnished with elegance and style, featuring marble bathrooms and balconies with city views. The resort also has a spa, a fitness centre, and a business centre. The resort has two restaurants and bars, including La Terrazza dell'Ambasciatori, which offers a panoramic view of Rome from its rooftop terrace.

Hotel Recommendations

Below are some hotel recommendations in Rome, based on different categories and criteria:

Best 5-Star Hotel In Rome: If you are looking for a lavish and elegant stay in the Eternal City, you can't go wrong with **Hotel de Russie**, A Rocco Forte Hotel. This hotel is located near Piazza del Popolo and features a chic and modern design, a two-tiered secret garden, a spa, and a Michelin-starred restaurant. The hotel also attracts celebrities and beautiful people who flock to its Stravinskij Bar and Le Jardin de Russie.

Best Boutique Hotel In Rome: If you prefer a more intimate and cosy experience, you can opt for **Hotel Vilòn**, a boutique hotel located near the Spanish Steps. This hotel is housed in a historical building that was once the residence of a noble family. The hotel has 18 rooms and suites, each with its unique style and personality. The hotel also has a charming courtyard, a library, and a restaurant that serves contemporary Italian cuisine.

Best Hotel For Romance In Rome: If you are travelling with your partner and want to enjoy some romance in Rome, you can book a room at **Hotel Eden**, Dorchester Collection. This hotel is located near Villa Borghese and offers a stunning view of the city from its rooftop terrace. The hotel has 98 rooms and suites, decorated with elegance and sophistication. The hotel also has a spa, a fitness centre, and two restaurants, including La Terrazza dell'Eden, which offers a panoramic view of Rome from its rooftop terrace.

Hotel With the Best Location In Rome: If you want to be close to the main attractions and landmarks in Rome, you can check in at **Chapter Roma,** a trendy hotel located near Campo de Fiori. This hotel is housed in a 19th-century building that was once a bank. The hotel has 42 rooms and suites, with industrial-chic decor and modern amenities. The hotel also has a cocktail bar, a restaurant that serves international cuisine, and a rooftop terrace that hosts events and parties.

Hostel Recommendations

Below are some hostel recommendations in Rome, based on different categories and criteria:

Best Hostel for Solo Travellers in Rome: **The RomeHello Hostel** is a friendly and social hostel that welcomes solo travellers from all over the world. The hostel has a cosy and colourful design, with spacious dorms and private rooms, all with en-suite bathrooms. The hostel also has a large common area with a bar, a kitchen, a library, and a games room. The hostel organizes daily activities and events, such as yoga classes, live music, pub crawls, and walking tours. The hostel is located near the Trevi Fountain and the Spanish Steps and is easily accessible by public transport.

Best Hostel for Digital Nomads in Rome: Ostello Bello Roma Colosseo is a modern and stylish hostel that caters to digital nomads and remote workers. The hostel has a co-working space with desks, chairs, printers, scanners, and free Wi-Fi. The hostel also has a rooftop terrace with a stunning view of the Colosseum, where you can relax and network with other guests. The hostel offers free breakfast, free snacks and drinks throughout the day, free pasta every evening, and free tours and activities. The hostel is located near the Colosseum and the Roman Forum and is well connected by metro and bus.

Best Hostel for Couples in Rome: The Bricks Rome is a boutique hostel that offers a romantic and cosy stay for couples. The hostel has 11 rooms, each with its theme and personality. The rooms are decorated with vintage furniture, artwork, and plants. The rooms also have private bathrooms, air conditioning, smart TVs, and mini-fridges. The hostel has a charming garden where you can enjoy breakfast or a glass of wine. The hostel is located near the Vatican City and the Castel Sant'Angelo, and is close to many restaurants and bars.

Best Party Hostel in Rome: **YellowSquare Rome** is a lively and fun hostel that is perfect for party animals. The hostel has a bar, a club, a restaurant, and a hair salon on-site, where you can enjoy drinks, music, food, and pampering. The hostel also has a gym, a kitchen, a laundry room, and a cinema room. The hostel organizes daily parties and events, such as karaoke nights, beer pong tournaments, DJ sets, and themed parties. The hostel is located near the Termini Station and is surrounded by many pubs and clubs.

Bed and Breakfast Recommendations

Bed and breakfasts are a great option for travellers who want to enjoy a cosy and authentic stay in Rome, with a personal touch and a friendly atmosphere. Bed and breakfasts are usually located in residential areas, away from the tourist crowds, but still close to the main attractions and public transport. Bed and breakfasts also offer a delicious breakfast every morning, which may include local specialities such as cornetti (croissants), cappuccino, and fresh fruit. Below are some bed and breakfast recommendations in Rome, based on different categories and criteria:

Best Bed and Breakfast for Solo Travelers in Rome: If you are travelling alone and want to meet other travellers and locals, you can choose **The Beehive**, a cosy and eco-friendly bed and breakfast near Termini Station. The Beehive has 12 rooms, ranging from dorms to private rooms, all with shared bathrooms. The Beehive also has a garden, a lounge, a kitchen, and a cafe. The Beehive organizes events and activities, such as yoga classes, cooking classes, wine tastings, and walking tours.

Best Bed and Breakfast for Families in Rome: If you are travelling with your family and want to have a comfortable and spacious stay in Rome, you can opt for **A Casa di Serena**, a charming bed and breakfast near Vatican City. A Casa di Serena has six rooms, each with its theme and personality. The rooms can accommodate up to four people, and have private bathrooms, air conditioning, TV, and Wi-Fi. A Casa di Serena also has a terrace where you can enjoy breakfast or relax.

Best Bed and Breakfast for Couples in Rome: If you are travelling with your partner and want to enjoy some romance in Rome, you can book a room at **Relais Maddalena**, a luxury bed and breakfast near Piazza Navona. Relais Maddalena has seven rooms, each with its style and elegance. The rooms have private bathrooms, air conditioning, TV, minibar, and Wi-Fi. Some rooms also have balconies or terraces with city views. Relais Maddalena also offers a continental breakfast served in your room or on the terrace.

Best Bed and Breakfast for Budget Travelers in Rome: If you are travelling on a budget and want to save some money without compromising on quality, you can stay at **Dreaming Rome**, a modern and colourful bed and breakfast near the Colosseum. Dreaming Rome has four rooms, each with four beds (two bunk beds). The rooms have shared bathrooms, air conditioning, lockers, and Wi-Fi. Dreaming Rome also has a common area with a kitchen, a TV, and a computer. Dreaming Rome also offers free breakfast, free pasta every evening, free coffee and tea all day, and free tours and activities.

Best Bed and Breakfast for Luxury Travelers in Rome: If you want to splurge on a lavish and elegant stay in Rome, you can choose **Residenza Napoleone III**, a historic bed and breakfast located in an 18th-century palace near the Spanish Steps. Residenza Napoleone III has two suites, each with its antique furniture, artworks, frescoes, and fireplaces. The suites have private bathrooms, air conditioning, TV, DVD player, minibar, and Wi-Fi. Residenza Napoleone III also offers a gourmet breakfast served in your suite or on the rooftop terrace.

Apartment Recommendations

Apartments are usually located in residential areas, where you can experience the authentic and local lifestyle of the city. Apartments also offer more space, amenities, and facilities than hotels, such as a kitchen, a living room, a washing machine, and Wi-Fi. Apartments are also more cost-effective than hotels, especially if you are travelling with a group or staying for a long time.

Many websites and platforms can help you find and book an apartment in Rome, such as Nestpick, Immobiliare.it, and Culture Trip. These websites allow you to search for apartments by location, price, size, type, and features. You can also read reviews, see photos, and contact the owners or agents directly. Some of the websites also offer additional services, such as airport transfers, cleaning services, and city guides.

Depending on your preferences, budget, and travel style, you can choose from different types of apartments in Rome, such as studios, lofts, penthouses, or villas. You can also choose from different areas and neighbourhoods in Rome, such as the historic centre, the Vatican City, Trastevere, Monti, or Testaccio. Each area has its charm and character, as well as its attractions and landmarks.

Below are some examples of apartments that you can rent in Rome:

Green Apartments Rome: These are four beautiful apartments located near the Colosseum and the Roman Forum. Each apartment has a double bedroom, a living room, a kitchen, a bathroom, and a satellite TV. The apartments are fully furnished and independent. The apartments also have free Wi-Fi and air conditioning.

Colosseo Apartments and Rooms: These are various types of apartments located near the Colosseum and Piazza Navona. The apartments are housed in historic buildings with elegant interiors. The apartments have private bathrooms, kitchens or kitchenettes, living rooms or sitting areas, and TVs. The apartments also have free Wi-Fi and air conditioning.

Chapter 8 • Outdoor Activities and Nature

Watersports in Rome

Rome may not be the first destination that comes to mind when you think of watersports, but the city and its surroundings offer some opportunities to enjoy water activities, such as kayaking, rafting, surfing, and sailing. Below are some of the watersports that you can try in Rome:

Kayaking: Kayaking is a great way to discover the hidden gems of Rome, such as the Tiber River, the Lake Albano, or the Lake Bracciano. You can paddle along the river and admire the monuments and bridges of the city, or enjoy the tranquillity and beauty of the lakes. You can also join a guided tour or a lesson that will provide you with equipment and instruction. Some of the places that offer kayaking in Rome are Watersports Center Roma, Rome Lake Kayaking Tour, and Roma Rafting.

Rafting: Rafting is a thrilling and adventurous activity that will take you on a ride along the rapids of a river. You can experience rafting in Rome on the Aniene River, a tributary of the Tiber that flows through a natural park. You can also join a guided tour or a lesson that will provide you with equipment and instruction. Some of the places that offer rafting in Rome are Roma Rafting, Aniene River Rafting, and River Tribe.

Surfing: Surfing is a fun and challenging activity that will test your balance and coordination on a board. You can surf in Rome on the Tyrrhenian Sea, which has some spots with good waves, especially during the winter months. You can also join a guided tour or a lesson that will provide you with equipment and instruction. Some of the places that offer surfing in Rome are Kitesurf-surf-sup-windsurf surf courses, Surf Club Lido di Ostia, and Surf School Roma.

Sailing: Sailing is a relaxing and enjoyable activity that will let you explore the sea and the coast of Rome. You can sail in Rome on the Tyrrhenian Sea, which has some beautiful islands and bays to visit, such as Ponza, Palmarola, or Fiumicino. You can also join a guided tour or a lesson that will provide you with equipment and instruction. Some of the places that offer sailing in Rome are Ponza Boat Trip, Capri Private Day Tour, and Sailing School Roma.

Exploring Parks, Zoos, and Gardens

Below are some of the ways you can experience the green side of Rome:

If you are interested in art and history, you can visit **Villa Borghese**, one of the largest and most beautiful parks in Rome. Villa Borghese was once the private estate of a noble family and now hosts several museums and monuments, such as the Galleria Borghese, the Museo Nazionale Etrusco, and the Temple of Asclepius. You can also admire the sculptures, fountains, and flowers that decorate the park, or rent a bike or a boat to explore it.

If you want to see some exotic animals and learn more about wildlife conservation, you can visit **Bioparco di Roma**, the oldest zoo in Italy. Bioparco di Roma hosts more than 1,000 animals from over 200 species, such as lions, tigers, elephants, giraffes, and monkeys. You can also enjoy some interactive exhibits, educational activities, and guided tours that will make your visit more fun and informative.

If you want to enjoy some stunning views of the city and its landmarks, you can visit **Giardino degli Aranci (the Orange Garden)** and **the Keyhole** on the Aventine Hill. Giardino degli Aranci is a small but charming garden that offers a panoramic view of Rome from its terrace. You can also smell the fragrance of the orange trees that give the garden its name. The Keyhole is a hidden gem that is located on the same hill, near the church of Santa Sabina. It is a small hole in a door that reveals a surprising view of St. Peter's Basilica framed by trees.

If you are looking for some adventure and adrenaline, you can visit **Parco degli Acquedotti (the Park of the Aqueducts),** part of the Appian Way Park and Rome's largest greenspace. Parco degli Acquedotti is a very peaceful place that features some ancient Roman aqueducts that run through it. You can also see some ruins of villas and tombs along the way. You can explore the park by walking, biking, or even horseback riding.

If you want to discover some hidden gems and botanical wonders, you can visit **Orto Botanico di Roma (the Botanical Garden of Rome),** run by Rome's first university La Sapienza. Orto Botanico di Roma is located in Trastevere, just outside of the heavy traffic. It hosts more than 3,000 plant species from different regions and climates, such as tropical, Mediterranean, alpine, and aquatic. You can also see some sculptures, fountains, and greenhouses that add to the beauty of the garden.

Beaches and Coastal Escapes

Below are some of the beaches and coastal experiences that you can try in Rome:

Lido di Ostia: This is the closest beach to Rome, only 30 minutes by train from the city centre. It is not the most beautiful or cleanest beach, but it is convenient and popular among locals and tourists alike. You can choose from a variety of stabilimenti (beach clubs) where you can rent a sunbed and an umbrella, or find a free spot on the public beach. You can also enjoy some food and drinks at the many bars and restaurants along the promenade.

Santa Marinella: This is a more pleasant and scenic beach than Ostia, about an hour by train from Rome. It has fine sand and calm water, protected by a breakwater. It is ideal for families with children, as well as for snorkelling and diving. You can also visit the nearby town of Santa Marinella, which has a charming harbour and a castle.

Sperlonga: This is one of the most beautiful and picturesque beach towns near Rome, about 90 minutes by train and bus from the city. It has two crescent-shaped beaches with clear blue water and white sand, surrounded by a rocky promontory. You can also explore the whitewashed old town, which has narrow alleys and stairs, or visit the nearby Grotto of Tiberius, where you can see some ancient Roman sculptures.

Fregene: This is a trendy beach near Rome, about an hour by bus from the city. It attracts a young and stylish crowd, who come here for its chic stabilimenti, its lively nightlife, and its water sports. You can surf, kite-surf, windsurf, or paddleboard here, or just relax on the sunbeds and enjoy the music and cocktails.

Ponza: This is a stunning island off the coast of Rome, about two hours by ferry from Anzio or Terracina. It is part of the Pontine Islands archipelago, which has a volcanic origin and a rich biodiversity. You can admire the colourful houses, the rocky cliffs, and the turquoise water of Ponza, or take a boat tour to explore its hidden coves and caves. You can also snorkel, scuba dive, or hike on the island.

Wellness: Spas, Retreats, and Yoga

Below are some of the wellness options that you can try in Rome:

Spas: Rome has many spas that offer various treatments and services, such as massages, facials, saunas, hammams, and more. You can enjoy a spa day in Rome in one of the many hotels, resorts, or independent centres that cater to your needs and preferences. Some of the best spas in Rome are the Spa at Trilussa Palace Hotel, Doma Luxury Spa, Caschera Spa, and Kami Spa.

Retreats: Rome has some retreats that offer holistic programs and activities, such as yoga, meditation, life coaching, and more. You can join a retreat in Rome to improve your physical, mental, and emotional well-being, as well as to learn new skills and meet new people. Some of the best retreats in Rome are YogAyur Gazometro, Stellatum, Artemís Spa, and Six Senses Rome.

Yoga: Rome has many yoga studios and centres that offer different styles and levels of yoga, such as hatha, vinyasa, Bikram, aerial, and more. You can practice yoga in Rome to enhance your flexibility, strength, balance, and awareness, as well as to reduce stress and tension. Some of the best yoga studios and centres in Rome are The Beehive, Nora Thai Massage Center, El Spa, and Baan Sabai.

Chapter 9 • Shopping in Rome

Fashion and Luxury Shopping

Below are some of the fashion and luxury shopping options that you can try in Rome:

If you want to shop at the most prestigious fashion houses in the world, you should head to **the Spanish Steps area**, where you will find the famous **Via dei Condotti** and its surrounding streets. Here you will find luxury brands like Gucci, Prada, Louis Vuitton, and Bulgari, as well as local designers like Valentino and Fendi. You can also admire the elegant window displays and the sophisticated atmosphere of this district.

If you prefer a more intimate and cosy shopping experience, you can visit **Monti**, one of the hippest neighbourhoods in Rome. Here you will find independent clothing brands, vintage shops, and art galleries, where you can discover unique and original fashion pieces. You can also enjoy some food and drinks at the trendy bars and restaurants along Via del Boschetto.

If you are looking for some bargains and discounts on designer labels, you can visit **Castel Romano Designer Outlet**, a shopping mall located about 25 km from Rome. Here you will find over 200 stores that offer up to 70% off on brands like Armani, Versace, Dolce & Gabbana, and Diesel. You can also enjoy some entertainment and dining options at this outlet.

If you want to experience some of the best Italian craftsmanship and quality, you can visit **Via del Governo Vecchio**, a charming street near Piazza Navona. Here you will find some of the best leather goods, jewellery, and accessories in Rome, made by local artisans and craftsmen. You can also find some vintage and antique items on this street.

If you want to splurge on some of the most exquisite and exclusive jewellery in Rome, you can visit **Via del Babuino**, a street near Piazza del Popolo. Here you will find some of the most renowned jewellers in Rome, such as Buccellati, Pomellato, Damiani, and Tiffany & Co. You can also admire some of the most beautiful artworks and sculptures on this street.

Local Markets and Souvenirs

Below are some of the local markets and souvenirs that you can try in Rome:

Campo de Fiori: This is one of the oldest and most famous markets in Rome, located in a lively square in the historic centre. Here you can find fresh fruits, vegetables, flowers, spices, cheese, and bread, as well as clothes, accessories, and souvenirs. You can also enjoy the atmosphere of the market, which is full of colours, sounds, and smells.

Porta Portese: This is the largest and most popular flea market in Rome, held every Sunday morning near Trastevere. Here you can find everything from clothes, shoes, bags, and jewelry, to books, records, posters, and cameras. You can also find some rare and valuable items, such as antique coins, furniture, and paintings. You need to bargain hard and watch out for pickpockets in this market.

Mercato delle Stampe: This is a speciality market that sells prints, books, maps, posters, and magazines. It is held every morning from Monday to Saturday near Largo della Fontanella di Borghese. Here you can find some rare and vintage prints of Rome and other cities, as well as some original artworks by famous artists.

Borghetto Flaminio: This is a chic and elegant market that sells designer clothes, accessories, and antiques. It is held every Sunday near Piazza del Popolo. Here you can find some pre-loved Prada, Gucci, Chanel, and Fendi items, as well as some fine jewellery and furniture. You need to pay a small entrance fee to access this market.

Mercato di Testaccio: This is a modern and vibrant market that sells food and street food. It is located in a covered building near the Pyramid of Cestius. Here you can find some of the best produce, meat, cheese, and fish in Rome, as well as some delicious snacks and dishes such as pizza al taglio (pizza by the slice), supplì (fried rice balls), and trapizzino (stuffed bread pockets).

Some of the best souvenirs that you can buy in Rome are:

Pecorino Romano cheese: This is a sheep-milk cheese that is typical of Rome and its region. It has a hard texture and a salty flavour. You can use it for cooking or eating with bread or fruit.

Leather goods: Rome has many shops and stalls that sell high-quality leather goods such as bags, wallets, belts, and jackets. You can find some handmade and customized items that will last for a long time.

Ceramic tiles: Rome has a long tradition of ceramic art that dates back to ancient times. You can find some beautiful ceramic tiles that depict scenes of Rome or other motifs. You can use them for decoration or as coasters.

Pinocchio dolls: Pinocchio is a famous character from an Italian fairy tale that was later adapted into a Disney movie. You can find some wooden Pinocchio dolls that are handcrafted and painted in different sizes and colours.

Espresso cups: Espresso is the quintessential Italian coffee that is served in small cups. You can buy some espresso cups that have different designs and patterns. You can also buy some coffee beans or ground coffee to make your espresso at home.

Artisan Crafts and Workshops

Below are some of the artisan crafts and workshops that you can try in Rome:

Leather: Rome has a long tradition of leather craftsmanship, dating back to ancient times. You can find some of the best leather goods in Rome, such as bags, wallets, belts, and jackets, made by local artisans and craftsmen. You can also visit some of the workshops where you can see how leather is cut, sewn, and dyed. Some of the places where you can find leather crafts and workshops in Rome are Funtiffany Arts & Crafts, which sells handmade leather items and offers courses on leather making; Watersports Center Roma, which sells and rents leather goods for water sports; and Via del Governo Vecchio, a street near Piazza Navona where you can find many leather shops and stalls.

Ceramics: Rome has a vibrant and colourful ceramic art scene, influenced by different cultures and styles. You can find some of the most beautiful ceramic tiles, plates, cups, and vases in Rome, decorated with various motifs and patterns. You can also visit some of the workshops where you can learn how to make your ceramic piece or paint an existing one. Some of the places where you can find ceramic crafts and workshops in Rome are Mercato delle Stampe, a market that sells prints, books, maps, posters, and ceramics; Vineyarts, a wine and art studio that offers courses on ceramic painting; and Via del Babuino, a street near Piazza del Popolo where you can find some of the most renowned ceramic shops.

Jewellery: Rome has a dazzling and elegant jewellery scene, ranging from classic to contemporary styles. You can find some of the most exquisite and exclusive jewellery in Rome, made with gold, silver, pearls, gems, and other materials. You can also visit some of the workshops where you can see how jewellery is designed, crafted, and polished. Some of the places where you can find jewellery crafts and workshops in Rome are Via dei Condotti, a street near the Spanish Steps where you can find some of the most prestigious jewellers in the world; The Traditional Artisans of Rome, a tour that takes you to some of the best jewellery shops and workshops in Rome; and Ostello Bello Roma Colosseo, a hostel that offers courses on jewellery making.

Prints: Rome has a fascinating and diverse print scene, inspired by its history and culture. You can find some of the most rare and vintage prints of Rome and other cities, as well as some original artworks by famous artists. You can also visit some of the workshops where you can learn how to make your print or buy one as a souvenir. Some of the places where you can find print crafts and workshops in Rome are Botteghiamo, a project that promotes and highlights the artisanal scene in Rome through tours, events, classes, and performances; YogAyur Gazometro, a yoga studio that offers courses on printmaking; and Parco degli Acquedotti, a park that hosts an annual festival of printmaking.

Antique and Vintage Shopping

Below are some of the best places to go for antique and vintage shopping in Rome:

Via del Governo Vecchio: This is a charming street near Piazza Navona, where you can find many antique shops and stalls that sell a variety of items, such as leather goods, prints, books, lamps, and mirrors. You can also find some vintage clothing and accessories at SiTenne Vintage Store, which sells handmade leather items and offers courses on leather making. This street is also a good place to find some hidden gems and bargains, as well as to enjoy the atmosphere of the old Rome.

Via dei Coronari: This is another beautiful street near Piazza Navona, where you can find some of the most prestigious and elegant antique shops in Rome. Here you can find some of the finest furniture, paintings, sculptures, and silverware in Rome, as well as some rare and valuable items such as coins, medals, and clocks. You can also visit some of the art galleries and museums that are located on this street, such as Galleria Carlo Maria Biagiarelli, which sells prints, books, maps, posters, and ceramics.

Via Cola di Rienzo: This is a popular shopping street near the Vatican City, where you can find some of the best fashion and luxury shops in Rome. However, you can also find some antique and vintage shops on this street, such as Vintage Market & Co., which sells clothes, shoes, bags, jewellery, and more. You can also visit Mercato delle Stampe, a market that sells prints, books, maps, posters, and ceramics.

Porta Portese: This is the largest and most famous flea market in Rome, held every Sunday morning near Trastevere. Here you can find everything from clothes, shoes, bags, and jewellery to books, records, posters, and cameras. You can also find some rare and valuable items such as antique coins, furniture, and paintings. However, you need to bargain hard and watch out for pickpockets in this market.

Mercatino Capannelle: This is a chic and elegant market that sells designer clothes, accessories, and antiques. It is held every Sunday near Ciampino Airport. Here you can find some pre-loved Prada, Gucci, Chanel, and Fendi items as well as some fine jewellery and furniture. You need to pay a small entrance fee to access this market.

Chapter 10 • Practical Information

Health and Safety Tips

Rome is a wonderful city to visit, but like any other destination, it has some health and safety risks that one should be aware of and prepared for. Below are some health and safety tips to take note of while visiting Rome:

Health: Rome has a good public health system and many private clinics and hospitals that offer quality medical care. However, it is advisable to have travel insurance that covers medical expenses and repatriation in case of emergency. You can also bring a European Health Insurance Card (EHIC) if you are from the EU, which will allow you to access public health services for free or at a reduced cost. If you need to see a doctor or go to a pharmacy, you can ask your hotel or hostel for recommendations, or use the online service Doctor in Italy, which connects you with English-speaking doctors and pharmacists in Rome. You can also call the emergency numbers 112 (general), 118 (ambulance), or

113 (police) if you need urgent assistance. Some of the common health issues that travellers may face in Rome are dehydration, sunburn, heatstroke, food poisoning, and allergies. To prevent these problems, you should drink plenty of water, wear sunscreen and a hat, avoid excessive alcohol consumption, eat at reputable places, and avoid contact with animals or plants that may cause allergic reactions.

Safety: Rome is generally a safe city for travellers it has some crime and security risks that travellers should be aware of and avoid. The most common crimes that affect tourists are pickpocketing, bag-snatching, and scams. To protect yourself from these crimes, you should stay alert, especially in crowded places and public transport, keep your valuables close to you or in a safe place, and avoid carrying large amounts of cash or expensive items. You should also be wary of strangers who approach you with offers, requests, or distractions, as they may be trying to rob you or trick you into paying for something you don't want or need. Some of the places where these crimes are more frequent are Termini Station, the Colosseum, the Vatican City, Piazza Navona, and Campo de' Fiori. Another safety risk that travellers may face in Rome is traffic accidents. Rome has a chaotic and congested traffic system, with many drivers who do not respect the rules or the pedestrians. To avoid getting hit by a car, scooter, or bus, you should always cross the street at designated crossings, look both ways before crossing, and follow the traffic lights and signs. You should also be careful when riding a bike or a scooter in Rome, as they may not have dedicated lanes or paths.

Emergency Contacts

Below are some of the emergency contacts that you should know before visiting Rome:

The general number for all emergencies in Italy is **113**. This number connects you to the state police (Polizia di Stato), who will assist you with any kind of emergency, such as accidents, thefts, or violence. They will also redirect your call to the appropriate service if needed.

The European emergency number is **112**. This number can be used to reach any emergency service in the European Union, such as police, fire, or ambulance. You can call this number for free from any phone, and the operators should speak English.

The number for urgent and emergency medical attention is **118**. This number connects you to the emergency health service (Emergenza Sanitaria), which will send an ambulance or a doctor to your location. They will also assign a colour code to your situation, depending on the severity and urgency.

The number for the fire brigade (Vigili del Fuoco) is **115**. This number can be used to report fires, weather emergencies, or other situations that require rescue or assistance. The fire brigade also deals with searches, rescues, and first-response operations.

The number for the Coast Guard (Guardia Costiera) is **1530**. This number can be used to report emergencies at sea, such as boat accidents, drownings, or pollution. The Coast Guard also provides information and assistance to sailors and tourists.

The Covid-19 hotline is **1500** (in Italy) or +39-02-3200 8345 or +39-02-8390 5385 (outside Italy). This number can be used to report symptoms, get tested, or ask for information about the coronavirus pandemic in Italy.

The number for urgent but non-emergency medical advice is **+39-06 570 600** (general line) or +39-06 7730 6650, +39-06 7730 6112, or +39-06 7730 6113 (English speaking). This number connects you to the medical guard (Guardia Medica), who will provide you with medical advice or assistance over the phone or at your location.

These are some of the main emergency contacts that you should know in Rome. However, there may be other numbers or services that are specific to your situation or location. Therefore, it is advisable to have travel insurance that covers medical expenses and repatriation in case of emergency. You can also ask your hotel or hostel for recommendations or assistance if you need help.

Communication and Internet Access

Below are some of the ways you can communicate and access the internet in Rome:

Phone: The country code for Italy is **+39**, and the area code for Rome is **06**. You can make local or international calls from public phones, which are located in various places such as airports, train stations, or post offices. You can use coins, prepaid cards, or credit cards to pay for the calls. You can also use your mobile phone in Rome, but you may need to check with your provider if your phone is compatible with the Italian network and what are the roaming charges. Alternatively, you can buy a local SIM card from one of the main operators in Italy, such as TIM, Vodafone, Wind Tre, or Iliad. You can find SIM cards at phone shops, newsstands, or supermarkets. You may need to show your passport or ID card to activate the SIM card.

Internet: The internet speed and coverage in Italy are improving, but they may not be as fast or reliable as in other European countries. You can access the internet in Rome through various options, such as Wi-Fi, mobile data, or internet cafes. Wi-Fi is widely available in Rome, especially in hotels, restaurants, cafes, and bars. However, some places may require you to register or pay a fee to use their Wi-Fi. You can also find some free public Wi-Fi hotspots in Rome, such as at airports, train stations, museums, or parks. Mobile data is another option to access the internet in Rome, but you may need to check with your provider if your plan includes data roaming and what are the costs. You can also buy a local SIM card with a data plan from one of the Italian operators1. Internet cafes are less common in Rome than before, but you can still find some places that offer Internet access and other services, such as printing or scanning. Some of the places where you can find internet cafes in Rome are Watersports Center Roma, Rome Lake Kayaking Tour, and Roma Rafting.

Chapter 11 •
Recommended Itineraries

One day in Rome

Rome is a city that offers so much to see and do, that one day is hardly enough to scratch the surface. However, if you only have 24 hours to explore the Eternal City, below are some suggestions on how to make the most of your time and enjoy a taste of its rich history, culture, and cuisine.

Morning: **Ancient Rome** Start your day with a visit to the Colosseum. You can buy tickets online in advance to skip the long lines or join a guided tour to learn more about the history and secrets of this impressive monument. Next, walk along the Via Sacra to the Roman Forum. Don't miss Palatine Hill. Here you can see the remains of palaces, gardens, and stadiums that belonged to emperors and aristocrats.

Afternoon: Vatican City After exploring ancient Rome, hop on the metro and head to Vatican City. You will need at least a few hours to visit the Vatican Museums where you can admire masterpieces by

Michelangelo, Raphael, Leonardo da Vinci, and many others. The highlight of the museum is the Sistine Chapel. From there, you can access St. Peter's Basilica, the largest and most important church in Christendom. If you have time and energy, you can also climb up to the dome of the Basilica for a stunning view of St. Peter's Square and Rome.

Evening: Trastevere After a long day of sightseeing, you deserve a relaxing evening in one of Rome's most charming neighbourhoods: Trastevere.

This is just a sample itinerary for one day in Rome. Of course, there are many other attractions and activities that you can choose from depending on your interests and preferences. No matter how long you stay or how many times you return, you will always find something new and exciting to discover.

Three days in Rome

Below is a suggested itinerary for three days in Rome, that will give you a taste of its history, culture, and cuisine.

Day 1: Ancient Rome and Vatican City Start your day with a visit to the Colosseum. Next, walk along the

Via Sacra to the Roman Forum. Don't miss Palatine Hill, where Romulus founded Rome in the 8th century BC. After exploring ancient Rome, hop on the metro and head to Vatican City. From there, you can access St. Peter's Basilica. For dinner, you can choose from a variety of restaurants near Vatican City or in Prati district.

Day 2: Baroque Rome and Trastevere On your second day, you can explore some of the most beautiful squares and fountains of Rome. Start from Piazza del Popolo, where you can see two identical churches (Santa Maria dei Miracoli and Santa Maria in Montesanto), an Egyptian obelisk (the oldest and tallest in Rome), and three fountains. From there, you can walk up to Pincio Hill Gardens for a panoramic view of Rome. Then head to Piazza di Spagna, where you can admire the Spanish Steps (the widest staircase in Europe) and the Barcaccia Fountain (shaped like a sinking boat). Next, walk along Via dei Condotti (the most famous shopping street in Rome) to reach Piazza Colonna, where you can see a column dedicated to Emperor Marcus Aurelius. Continue to Piazza di Pietra (Stone Square), where you can see 11 columns from an ancient temple dedicated to Emperor Hadrian. From there, walk to Piazza della

Rotonda (Rotunda Square), where you can see one of the best-preserved ancient buildings in Rome: the Pantheon. Next to the Pantheon is Piazza della Minerva (Minerva Square), where you can see an elephant statue holding an obelisk designed by Bernini. After visiting these squares, you might want to take a break at one of the many cafés or gelaterias nearby. Some of the best ones are Sant'Eustachio Il Caffè (famous for its coffee), Giolitti (one of the oldest gelaterias in Rome), Tazza d'Oro (another coffee institution), and Gelateria del Teatro (known for its creative flavours).

In the afternoon, you can visit Piazza Navona. You can also see the Church of Sant'Agnese in Agone (built by Borromini) and the Palazzo Pamphilj (now the Brazilian Embassy). Piazza Navona is a great place to enjoy an aperitivo (a pre-dinner drink with snacks) or watch street performers and artists. From Piazza Navona, you can cross the Tiber River and enter Trastevere.

Day 3: Museums, Parks, and Nightlife On your third day, you can visit some of the best museums and parks in Rome. Start with the Capitoline Museums, located on Capitoline Hill, one of the seven hills of Rome. Some of the highlights are the bronze statue of

Marcus Aurelius on horseback, the bronze statue of the she-wolf nursing Romulus and Remus (the symbol of Rome), the busts of Roman emperors and philosophers, the Dying Gaul (a masterpiece of Hellenistic sculpture), and the Capitoline Venus (a copy of a famous Greek statue). From the museums, you can also enjoy a stunning view of the Roman Forum from a terrace.

After visiting the museums, you can walk to Villa Borghese, the largest and most popular park in Rome. Among its attractions are: the Borghese Gallery (a museum that houses a superb collection of paintings and sculptures by artists such as Caravaggio, Bernini, Titian, Raphael, and Canova), the landscaped Giardino del Lago (Lake Garden) with a temple dedicated to Aesculapius (the god of medicine), Piazza di Siena (a dusty arena used for equestrian events), and a panoramic terrace on Pincio Hill. You can also rent a bike or a boat to explore the park.

In the evening, you can experience some of the best nightlife in Rome. Depending on your mood and preferences, you can choose from different options. If you want to go clubbing, you can head to Testaccio district, where you can find some of the most popular clubs in Rome. Some of them are Akab Club (a trendy club that plays different genres of music), L'Alibi Club (one of the oldest gay clubs in Rome), Goa Club (a stylish club that hosts international DJs), Rashomon Club (an underground club that plays techno and electronic music), and La Cabala Club (an exclusive club that attracts a glamorous crowd). If you want to enjoy live music, you can head to the San Lorenzo district, where you can find some of the best venues for rock, jazz, blues, indie, and alternative music. Some of them are Circolo degli Artisti (a cultural centre that hosts concerts, exhibitions, and events), Sinister Noise Club (a club that plays rock and metal music), Monk Club (a club that hosts emerging bands and DJs), Big Mama Club (a club that plays blues and soul music), and Fonclea Pub (a pub that plays jazz and acoustic music). If you want to have a more laid-back night out, you can head to Monti district, where you can find some of the coolest bars in Rome.

Five days in Rome

If you have five days to explore the Eternal City, below is a suggested itinerary that will help you make the most of your time.

Day 1: Ancient Rome Start your trip with a visit to the Colosseum. Next, walk to the nearby Roman Forum. For lunch, head to the Monti neighbourhood, where you can find a variety of restaurants, cafes, and bars to suit your taste and budget. In the afternoon, continue your exploration of ancient Rome with a visit to the Pantheon. Then, stroll around the Piazza Navona, one of the most beautiful squares in Rome, where you can admire the fountains, sculptures, and churches. End your day with a dinner at one of the many restaurants in the area, or treat yourself to gelato at the Giolitti ice cream parlour.

Day 2: Vatican City On your second day, dedicate your time to visiting the Vatican City, the smallest and holiest state in the world, home to the Pope and some of the most important art collections in history. The highlight of your visit will be the Sistine Chapel, where you can gaze at the ceiling frescoes painted by Michelangelo, depicting scenes from the Bible. For lunch, you can either eat at one of the cafeterias inside the museums or go outside and find a nearby restaurant or pizzeria. In the afternoon, you can either continue your visit to the museums or explore other attractions in the Vatican City, such as the Vatican Gardens, the Castel

Sant'Angelo, or the St. Peter's Square. For dinner, you can either stay in the area or go back to Rome and enjoy a night out in one of its lively neighbourhoods.

Day 3: Art and Culture On your third day, immerse yourself in the art and culture of Rome with a visit to some of its most famous museums and galleries. You can start your day with a visit to the Galleria Borghese. For lunch, you can either eat at one of the cafes inside the park or go outside and find a restaurant nearby. In the afternoon, you can continue your cultural tour with a visit to one of these options:

The Capitoline Museums, where you can see ancient Roman sculptures, paintings, coins, and more.

The National Roman Museum, where you can see archaeological finds from different periods of Roman history.

The MAXXI Museum, where you can see contemporary art and architecture exhibitions.

The Galleria Nazionale d'Arte Moderna, where you can see modern artworks by artists such as Monet, Van Gogh, Klimt, Modigliani, and more. For dinner, you can either stay in the area or go back to Rome and enjoy a night out in one of its lively neighbourhoods.

Day 4: Romantic Rome On your fourth day, experience the romantic side of Rome with a visit to some of its most charming attractions. You can start your day with a visit to the Trevi Fountain. Next, walk to the nearby Spanish Steps. You can also shop at some of the luxury boutiques and stores in the area, such as Prada, Gucci, Valentino, and more. For lunch, you can either eat at one of the restaurants or cafes in the area or go to the Campo de' Fiori, a lively market square where you can find fresh produce, flowers, spices, and more. In the afternoon, you can continue your romantic tour with a visit to one of these options:

The Villa Farnesina is a Renaissance villa decorated with frescoes by Raphael and other artists.

The Aventine Hill is one of the seven hills of Rome, where you can see the Orange Garden, the Rose Garden, and the Keyhole View of St. Peter's Basilica.

The Trastevere neighbourhood is one of the most picturesque and authentic areas of Rome, where you can stroll along the cobblestone streets, see the medieval churches, and enjoy the nightlife.

The Tiber River, where you can take a boat cruise or walk along the banks and see the bridges, monuments, and islands. For dinner, you can either stay in the area or go back to Rome and enjoy a night out in one of its lively neighbourhoods.

Day 5: Day Trip On your fifth and final day, you can take a day trip to one of the many destinations near Rome that offer a different perspective and experience of Italy. You can choose from one of these options:

Ostia Antica is an ancient Roman port city that preserves the ruins of temples, theatres, baths, houses, and more.

Tivoli is a town that hosts two UNESCO World Heritage Sites: the Villa d'Este, a Renaissance villa with gardens and fountains, and the Villa Adriana, an imperial palace with pools and sculptures.

Naples, a vibrant city that is famous for its pizza, coffee, art, and culture, as well as its proximity to the Pompeii archaeological site and the Mount Vesuvius volcano.

Florence is a city that is considered the birthplace of the Renaissance and that boasts some of the most iconic landmarks in Italy, such as the Duomo, the Uffizi Gallery, the Ponte Vecchio, and more.

To make your day trip easier and more enjoyable, you can book a guided tour or a train ticket online or at one of the stations in Rome. Make sure to check the schedules and prices before you go. For lunch, you can either eat at one of the restaurants or cafes in your destination or bring your food. In the evening, you can return to Rome and pack your bags for your departure.

This is a summary of a possible five-day itinerary for Rome. You can adjust it according to your preferences, budget, and time. Have a wonderful time in Rome!

Seven days in Rome

If you have seven days to explore the Eternal City, below is a suggested itinerary that will help you make the most of your time.

Day 1: Ancient Rome Start your trip with a visit to the Colosseum. You can book a guided tour or an audio guide to learn more about the history and secrets of this impressive structure. Next, walk to the nearby Roman Forum. You can also climb up to the Palatine Hill, where the emperors and aristocrats lived, and enjoy a panoramic view of the city. For lunch, head to the Monti neighbourhood, where you can find a variety of restaurants, cafes, and bars to suit your taste and budget. In the afternoon, continue your exploration of ancient Rome with a visit to the Pantheon. Then, stroll around the Piazza Navona, one of the most beautiful squares in Rome, where you can admire the fountains, sculptures, and churches. End your day with a dinner at one of the many restaurants in the area, or treat yourself to gelato at the Giolitti ice cream parlour.

Day 2: Vatican City On your second day, dedicate your time to visiting the Vatican City. You can start your day early and join a queue to enter the St. Peter's Basilica. Next, head to the Vatican Museums. For lunch, you can either eat at one of the cafeterias inside the museums or go outside and find a nearby restaurant or pizzeria. In the afternoon, you can either continue your visit to the museums or explore other attractions in the Vatican City, such as the Vatican Gardens, the Castel Sant'Angelo, or the St. Peter's Square. For dinner, you can either stay in the area or go back to Rome and enjoy a night out in one of its lively neighbourhoods.

Day 3: Art and Culture On your third day, immerse yourself in the art and culture of Rome with a visit to some of its most famous museums and galleries. You can start your day with a visit to the Galleria Borghese. For lunch, you can either eat at one of the cafes inside the park or go outside and find a restaurant nearby. In the afternoon, you can continue your cultural tour with a visit to one of these options:

The Capitoline Museums, where you can see ancient Roman sculptures, paintings, coins, and more.

The National Roman Museum, where you can see archaeological finds from different periods of Roman history.

The MAXXI Museum, where you can see contemporary art and architecture exhibitions.

The Galleria Nazionale d'Arte Moderna, where you can see modern artworks by artists such as Monet, Van Gogh, Klimt, Modigliani, and more. For dinner, you can either stay in the area or go back to Rome and enjoy a night out in one of its lively neighbourhoods.

Day 4: Romantic Rome On your fourth day, experience the romantic side of Rome with a visit to some of its most charming attractions. You can start your day with a visit to the Trevi Fountain. Next, walk to the nearby Spanish Steps. For lunch, you can either eat at one of the restaurants or cafes in the area or go to the

Campo de' Fiori, a lively market square where you can find fresh produce, flowers, spices, and more. In the afternoon, you can continue your romantic tour with a visit to one of these options:

The Villa Farnesina is a Renaissance villa decorated with frescoes by Raphael and other artists.

The Aventine Hill is one of the seven hills of Rome, where you can see the Orange Garden, the Rose Garden, and the Keyhole View of St. Peter's Basilica.

The Trastevere neighbourhood is one of the most picturesque and authentic areas of Rome, where you can stroll along the cobblestone streets, see the medieval churches, and enjoy the nightlife.

The Tiber River, where you can take a boat cruise or walk along the banks and see the bridges, monuments, and islands. For dinner, you can either stay in the area or go back to Rome and enjoy a night out in one of its lively neighbourhoods.

Day 5: Day Trip to Ostia Antica On your fifth day, you can take a day trip to Ostia Antica, an ancient Roman port city that preserves the ruins of temples, theatres, baths, houses, and more. You can reach Ostia Antica by train from Rome in about 30 minutes.

Day 6: Day Trip to Tivoli On your sixth day, you can take a day trip to Tivoli, a town that hosts two UNESCO World Heritage Sites: the Villa d'Este, a Renaissance villa with gardens and fountains, and the Villa Adriana, an imperial palace with pools and sculptures. You can reach Tivoli by bus or train from Rome in about an hour.

Day 7: Day Trip to Florence On your seventh and final day, you can take a day trip to Florence, a city that is considered the birthplace of the Renaissance and that boasts some of the most iconic landmarks in Italy, such as the Duomo, the Uffizi Gallery, the Ponte Vecchio, and more. You can reach Florence by train from Rome in about an hour and a half. In the evening, you can return to Rome and pack your bags for your departure.

This is a possible seven-day itinerary for Rome. You can adjust it according to your preferences, budget, and time. Have a wonderful time in Rome!

Chapter 12 • Travelling with Children

Family-Friendly Attractions

Below are some of the best family-friendly attractions in Rome:

Colosseum: The Colosseum is one of the most iconic and impressive monuments in Rome and a must-see for any visitor. Your kids will love to imagine what it was like to be a gladiator or a spectator in the Colosseum.

Vatican City: The Vatican City is the smallest and holiest state in the world. Your kids will be amazed by the beauty and variety of the artworks in the Vatican City.

Galleria Borghese: The Galleria Borghese is an artistic gem in Rome. Your kids will be fascinated by the realistic and expressive sculptures by Bernini, such as Apollo and Daphne or David.

Bioparco: The Bioparco is Rome's zoo, located in Villa Borghese. The Bioparco is a great place to learn about animals and their environments, as well as to have fun with your kids.

Pinocchio Store: The Pinocchio Store is a charming shop in Rome that sells wooden toys and puppets inspired by the famous story of Pinocchio. The Pinocchio Store is a magical place for kids and adults alike who love this classic tale.

Child-Friendly Accommodation

Rome is a wonderful destination for families. However, finding child-friendly accommodation in Rome can be challenging, as not all hotels and apartments are equipped to cater to the needs and preferences of families travelling with children. To help you with your search, we have compiled a list of some of the best child-friendly accommodations in Rome, based on their location, amenities, and facilities. Below are some of the options you can consider:

Hotel De Russie, Rocco Forte: This is a 5-star hotel located in the heart of Rome. The hotel has a beautiful garden with a fountain and a playground, where children can run and play. The hotel offers a range of services and amenities for families, such as babysitting, children's menus, playpens, high chairs, toys, books, games, DVDs, and more. The hotel also organizes activities and events for children, such as treasure hunts, cooking classes, art workshops, and more.

The Gran Melia: This is a 5-star hotel located on the banks of the Tiber River. The hotel offers a range of services and amenities for families, such as babysitting, children's menus, playpens, high chairs, toys, books, games, DVDs, and more. The hotel also has a kids club called Gladiator's Club, where children can enjoy activities such as arts and crafts, sports, games, and more.

The Rome Cavalieri: This is a 5-star hotel located on a hill overlooking Rome. The hotel has a large garden with three outdoor pools and a playground, where children can swim and play. The hotel offers a range of services and amenities for families, such as babysitting, children's menus, playpens, high chairs, toys, books, games, DVDs, and more. The hotel also has a kids club called IT Club, where children can enjoy activities such as painting, dancing, cooking, and more.

The Cosmopolita Hotel: This is a 4-star hotel located in the centre of Rome. The hotel offers a range of services and amenities for families, such as babysitting, children's menus, playpens, high chairs, toys, books, games, DVDs, and more.

Palazzo Navona Hotel: This is a 4-star hotel located in the heart of Rome. The hotel also offers a range of services and amenities for families, such as babysitting, children's menus, playpens, high chairs, toys, books, games, DVDs, and more.

These are some of the best child-friendly accommodations in Rome that you can choose from. They offer everything you need to make your stay in Rome comfortable and enjoyable for you and your kids.

Chapter 13 • Travelling on a Budget

Budget-Friendly Accommodation

Below are some of the options you can consider:

Hotel California: This is a 3-star hotel located near the Termini Train and Metro Station, which makes it easy and cheap to get around the city. The hotel offers air-conditioned rooms with flat-screen satellite TV and free WiFi throughout. The rooms also have private bathrooms with hairdryers and toiletries. The hotel has a 24-hour front desk, luggage storage, and a bar. The hotel is close to many attractions, such as the Colosseum, the Roman Forum, and the Basilica di Santa Maria Maggiore.

Soggiorno Downtown: This is a bed and breakfast located in the centre of Rome, near the Roman Forum and the Colosseum. The rooms are en suite and offer free WiFi and a flat-screen TV. The rooms also have air conditioning and a minibar. The bed and breakfast offers a continental breakfast served daily in your room. The bed and breakfast has a 24-hour front desk, luggage storage, and a terrace. The bed and breakfast is close to many attractions, such as the Trevi Fountain, the Pantheon, and the Piazza Navona.

These are some of the best budget-friendly accommodations in Rome that you can choose from. Have a wonderful time in Rome!

Cheap Eats and Local Food

Below are some of the best cheap eats and local food in Rome:

Pasta: You can enjoy this dish at many restaurants and trattorias in Rome, such as Pasta Chef, where you can choose your pasta type and sauce from a counter and watch it being cooked in front of you. A portion of pasta costs around €5-€6.

Pizza: Pizza is another staple food in Rome, and you can find it in different styles and varieties. One of the most common and cheap ways to eat pizza in Rome is pizza al taglio (pizza by the slice), which is sold by weight at many bakeries and pizzerias. You can choose from a wide range of toppings, such as cheese, tomato, ham, mushrooms, vegetables, and more. Some of the best places to try pizza al taglio are Pizza Zizza, where you can sample different kinds of pizza for €10-€15 per person, and Suppli, where you can also try the famous supply, fried rice balls stuffed with cheese and tomato sauce. A slice of pizza costs around €2-€4.

Sandwiches: Sandwiches are a great option for a quick and filling snack or meal in Rome, and you can find them in many shapes and sizes. You can try trapizzino, one of the most popular and delicious sandwiches in Rome at Trapizzino, where each sandwich costs €3.50 or €4. Another great sandwich option is porchetta, roasted pork seasoned with herbs and spices, sliced and stuffed into a crusty bread roll. You can try porchetta at Er Pizzicarolo or Porcadella, where each sandwich costs around €5.

Gelato: Gelato is the Italian word for ice cream, but it is not the same as the regular ice cream you may be used to. Gelato is made with fresh ingredients, less air, less fat, and more flavour than regular ice cream, resulting in a creamy and smooth texture and a rich taste. Gelato comes in many flavors, from classic ones like chocolate, vanilla, or pistachio, to more exotic ones like tiramisu, ricotta cheese with figs, or basil with lemon. You can find gelato shops all over Rome, but some of the best ones are Gelateria Il Dolce Sorriso, where you can try their signature dark chocolate flavour; Gelateria Azzaro, where you can taste their homemade gelato made with natural ingredients; and Sweet Life Gelateria Pasticceria Artigianale, where you can enjoy their gelato delivered with care and kindness. A cone or cup of gelato costs around €2-€4.

These are some of the best cheap eats and local food in Rome that you can try during your visit. They will give you a taste of authentic Roman cuisine without breaking the bank.

Free and Affordable Attractions

Below are some of the options you can consider:

Colosseum: The entrance fee is €16, but you can visit it for free on the first Sunday of every month.

Vatican City: The entrance to the basilica is free, but you have to pay €8 to access the dome. The entrance fee to the museums is €17, but you can visit them for free on the last Sunday of every month before 13:30.

Pantheon: The entrance to the Pantheon is free, but you can also book a guided tour or an audio guide for a small fee.

Piazza Navona: Visiting Piazza Navona is free, but you may want to buy a souvenir or a snack from one of the vendors.

Appia Antica Regional Park: Visiting Appia Antica Regional Park is free, but you may have to pay a small fee to enter some of the monuments or catacombs.

Transportation Tips for Saving Money

Below are some transportation tips you need to know to save money in Rome:

Buy a travel card or a Roma Pass: If you plan to use public transport frequently, it is cheaper and more convenient to buy a travel card or a Roma Pass than to pay for single tickets. A travel card gives you unlimited access to the metro, buses, and trams for a certain period, such as 24 hours (€7), 48 hours (€12.50), or 72 hours (€18). A Roma Pass is a tourist card that gives you free access to two museums and/or archaeological sites, discounted entry to other attractions, and unlimited use of public transport for 48 hours (€28) or 72 hours (€38.50). You can buy these cards at metro stations, tourist offices, or online.

Use public transport instead of taxis: Taxis can be expensive and unreliable in Rome, especially during peak hours or in busy areas. A better and cheaper alternative is to use public transport, which is fairly efficient and covers most of the city. You can use the metro, which has two lines (A and B) that intersect at

Termini station; the buses, which have a wide network of routes and stops; or the trams, which run on some of the main streets. You can also use the local trains, which are cheap and fast, to get to some of the nearby destinations, such as Ostia Antica or Tivoli.

Walk and explore: One of the best ways to save money on transportation in Rome is to walk! The city centre is relatively compact and easy to navigate by foot, and you can enjoy the sights and sounds of Rome along the way. You can also discover some hidden gems and off-the-beaten-path attractions that you might miss otherwise. Walking is also good for your health and the environment.

Rent a bike or a scooter: If you want to explore Rome in a more fun and adventurous way, you can rent a bike or a scooter and ride around the city. You can find many rental shops near the main attractions or online. A bike rental costs around €3 per hour or €15 per day; a scooter rental costs around €25 per day. You can also join a guided bike or scooter tour to see some of the highlights of Rome with an expert guide. However, be careful when riding in Rome, as the traffic can be chaotic and the roads can be uneven.

Chapter 14 • Day Trips and Excursions

Ostia Antica and the Roman coast

If you want to explore the ancient Roman port city and the beautiful Roman coast, you can take a day trip to Ostia Antica and the Lido di Ostia from Rome. Below is a guide on how to plan your trip and what to see and do.

How to get there: You can reach Ostia Antica and the Lido di Ostia by train from Rome in about 30 minutes. You can take the metro line B to Piramide station, then change to the Roma-Lido train that departs from the same station. You can buy a single ticket for €1.50 or a day pass for €7 that covers both the metro and the train. You can also buy a Roma Pass that gives you free access to public transport and some attractions for 48 hours (€28) or 72 hours (€38.50). To get off at Ostia Antica, you need to take the train that stops at every station and get off at Ostia Antica station. To get off at Lido di Ostia, you can take any train and get off at Lido Centro station or any of the following stations along the coast.

What to see and do: Ostia Antica is an archaeological site that preserves the ruins of temples, theatres, baths, houses, and more from the ancient Roman port city. You can explore the site at your own pace or join a guided tour. You can also visit the Ostia Antica Museum, where you can see artefacts and models from the site. The entrance fee to the site and the museum is €12, but you can visit it for free with a Roma Pass or on the first Sunday of every month. Lido di Ostia is a seaside resort where you can relax on the beach or enjoy some water activities. You can find both public and private beaches along the coast, as well as restaurants, cafes, bars, and shops. You can also visit some attractions in Lido di Ostia, such as the Castello di Giulio II, a 15th-century castle that overlooks the sea; the Borgo Marinaro, a picturesque fishing village with colourful boats; or the Parco Naturale Regionale del Litorale Romano, a natural park with dunes, pine forests, and wetlands.

Tips and recommendations: Below are some tips and recommendations to make your trip more enjoyable and affordable:

The best time to visit Ostia Antica and the Lido di Ostia is from April to October when the weather is warm and sunny. However, avoid going on weekends or public holidays, when the sites can be crowded and noisy.

Wear comfortable shoes, sunscreen, a hat, sunglasses, and water when visiting Ostia Antica, as the site is large and exposed to the sun. You can also bring your food or buy snacks at the vending machines inside the site.

Bring your swimsuit, towel, umbrella, and flip-flops when visiting Lido di Ostia, as you may want to swim or sunbathe on the beach. You can also rent sunbeds and umbrellas at some of the private beaches for a fee.

Try some of the local food in Ostia Antica and Lido di Ostia, such as pizza al taglio (pizza by the slice), suppli (fried rice balls stuffed with cheese and tomato sauce), or fritto misto (fried seafood). You can also enjoy some gelato or coffee at one of the many gelaterias or cafes.

Tivoli and the Villa d'Este

Tivoli and the Villa d'Este are two of the most beautiful and fascinating destinations near Rome, where you can enjoy the history, art, and nature of Italy. Below is a guide on how to plan your trip and what to see and do.

How to get there: You can reach Tivoli and the Villa d'Este by bus or train from Rome in about an hour. You can take the metro line B to Ponte Mammolo station, then change to the Cotral bus that departs from the same station. You can buy a single ticket for €2.20 or a day pass for €4.40 that covers both the metro and the bus. You can also buy a Roma Pass that gives you free access to public transport and some attractions for 48 hours (€28) or 72 hours (€38.50). To get off at Tivoli, you need to take the bus that stops at Largo Nazioni Unite or Piazza Garibaldi. To get off at the Villa d'Este, you need to take the bus that stops at Piazza Trento. Alternatively, you can take the train from Tiburtina station in Rome to Tivoli station. You can buy a single ticket for €2.60 or a day pass for €6 that covers both the train and the bus. You can also use your Roma Pass for the train. To get to the Villa d'Este from Tivoli station, you can take a local bus or walk for about 20 minutes.

What to see and do: Tivoli is an ancient town, dating back to the Roman times. You can visit some of its attractions, such as the Temple of Vesta, a circular temple dedicated to the goddess of the hearth; the Temple of Sibyl, a rectangular temple dedicated to the prophetess who foretold the birth of Christ; the Villa Gregoriana, a natural park with waterfalls, caves, and ruins; and the Rocca Pia, a 15th-century castle built by Pope Pius II. The Villa d'Este is one of the most remarkable examples of Renaissance culture, listed as a UNESCO World Heritage Site. It is a masterpiece of architecture and landscape design, famous for its splendid gardens and fountains. You can explore the villa and its gardens at your own pace or join a guided tour. You can also visit the Villa d'Este Museum, where you can see artefacts and models from the site.

Tips and recommendations: Below are some tips and recommendations to make your trip more enjoyable and affordable:

The best time to visit Tivoli and the Villa d'Este is from April to October when the weather is warm and sunny. However, avoid going on weekends or public holidays, when the sites can be crowded and noisy.

Wear comfortable shoes, sunscreen, a hat, sunglasses, and water when visiting Tivoli and the Villa d'Este, as the sites are large and exposed to the sun. You can also bring your food or buy snacks at the vending machines inside the sites.

The entrance fee to Tivoli is free, but you may have to pay a small fee to enter some of its attractions. The entrance fee to the Villa d'Este is €10, but you can visit it for free with a Roma Pass or on the first Sunday of every month.

Try some of the local food in Tivoli and the Villa d'Este, such as fraschette (rustic taverns that serve cheese, salami, bread, and wine), porchetta (roasted pork seasoned with herbs and spices), or ciambelle al vino (ring-shaped cookies made with wine).

Naples and Pompeii

Naples and Pompeii are two of the most fascinating and contrasting destinations near Rome, where you can experience the culture, history, and cuisine of southern Italy. Below is a guide on how to plan your trip and what to see and do.

How to get there: You can reach Naples and Pompeii by train from Rome in about an hour and a half. You can take the high-speed train from Roma Termini station to Napoli Centrale station, which costs around €40-€50 for a one-way ticket. You can also take the regional train from Roma Tiburtina station to Napoli Centrale station, which costs around €10-€15 for a one-way ticket. You can buy your train tickets online or at the station. To get to Pompeii from Naples, you can take the Circumvesuviana train from Napoli Garibaldi station, which is located under Napoli Centrale station. The train takes about 30 minutes to reach Pompei Scavi station, which is right outside the entrance to the archaeological site. The train ticket costs €3.60 for a one-way trip.

What to see and do: Naples is the third-largest city in Italy and one of the oldest and most vibrant cities in Europe. It has a rich and diverse culture, influenced by its Greek, Roman, Norman, Spanish, French, and Bourbon past. You can visit some of its attractions, such as:

The Historic Centre is a UNESCO World Heritage Site that preserves the ancient streets, churches, palaces, and monuments of Naples. You can stroll along the

Spaccanapoli, the main street that divides the city in two; admire the Duomo, the cathedral that houses the relics of San Gennaro, the patron saint of Naples; see the Gesù Nuovo, a 16th-century church with a unique facade; or explore the Naples Underground, a network of tunnels and chambers that date back to the Greek and Roman times.

The National Archaeological Museum is one of the most important and impressive museums in Italy, where you can see a vast collection of artefacts from Pompeii, Herculaneum, and other ancient sites. You can marvel at the Farnese Collection, which includes sculptures such as the Farnese Hercules and the Farnese Bull; admire the Mosaics Collection, which features stunning works such as the Alexander Mosaic and the Cave Canem Mosaic; or explore the Secret Cabinet, which displays erotic art and objects from Pompeii.

The Castel dell'Ovo is a medieval castle that stands on a small island in the Bay of Naples. It is the oldest castle in Naples and offers a panoramic view of the city and the sea. You can visit the castle for free and see its towers, courtyards, and halls; or enjoy a meal or a drink at one of the restaurants or bars on the island.

Pompeii is an archaeological site that preserves the ruins of an ancient Roman city that was destroyed by the eruption of Mount Vesuvius in 79 BC. It is one of the most visited and best-preserved sites in the world, where you can see what life was like in Roman times. You can visit some of its attractions, such as:

The Amphitheatre, the oldest surviving Roman amphitheatre, where gladiator fights, animal hunts, and other spectacles took place. You can walk around the arena, the seats, and the corridors of the amphitheatre; or imagine the cheers and boos of the crowd.

The Houses, where you can see how Pompeians lived, worked, and entertained themselves. You can visit some of the most famous and luxurious houses, such as the House of the Faun, the House of the Vettii, or the House of the Tragic Poet; or see some of the most common and modest houses, such as the House of Menander, the House of Pansa, or the House of Sallust.

Tips and recommendations: Below are some tips and recommendations to make your trip more enjoyable and affordable:

The best time to visit Naples and Pompeii is from April to June or from September to October when the weather is mild and sunny. However, avoid going on weekends or public holidays, when the sites can be crowded and noisy.

Wear comfortable shoes, sunscreen, a hat, sunglasses, and water when visiting Naples and Pompeii, as the sites are large and exposed to the sun. You can also bring your food or buy snacks at the vending machines inside the sites.

The entrance fee to Naples is free, but you may have to pay a small fee to enter some of its attractions. The entrance fee to Pompeii is €15, but you can visit it for free with a Roma Pass or on the first Sunday of every month.

Try some of the local food in Naples and Pompeii, such as pizza (Naples is the birthplace of pizza), sfogliatella (a pastry filled with ricotta cheese and candied fruit), baba (a cake soaked in rum syrup), or limoncello (a lemon liqueur).

Florence and the Uffizi Gallery

Florence and the Uffizi Gallery are two of the most attractive and inspiring destinations in Italy, where you can admire the beauty and genius of the Renaissance. Below is a guide on how to plan your trip and what to see and do.

How to get there: You can reach Florence and the Uffizi Gallery by train from Rome in about an hour and a half. You can take the high-speed train from Roma Termini station to Firenze Santa Maria Novella station, which costs around €40-€50 for a one-way ticket. You can also take the regional train from Roma Tiburtina station to Firenze Campo di Marte station, which costs around €10-€15 for a one-way ticket. You can buy your train tickets online or at the station. To get to the Uffizi Gallery from Florence, you can walk for about 15 minutes along the historic centre, or take a bus or a taxi to Piazzale degli Uffizi.

What to see and do: Florence is the capital of Tuscany and one of the most beautiful and cultural cities in Europe. It was the birthplace and the cradle of the Renaissance, a period of artistic, scientific, and humanistic flourishing that changed the course of history. You can visit some of its attractions, such as:

The Duomo, the cathedral of Florence, is one of the largest and most impressive churches in the world. It is famous for its dome, designed by Brunelleschi, and its bell tower, designed by Giotto. You can climb up to the top of the dome or the tower for a stunning view of the city.

The Ponte Vecchio, the oldest and most picturesque bridge in Florence, which crosses the Arno River. It is lined with shops selling jewellery, art, and souvenirs. You can also see the Vasari Corridor, a secret passage that connects the Uffizi Gallery with the Pitti Palace, built by Vasari for Cosimo I de' Medici.

The Piazza della Signoria, the main square and the political heart of Florence, where you can admire the Palazzo Vecchio, the town hall that houses a museum and a tower; the Loggia dei Lanzi, an open-air gallery that displays sculptures by Cellini, Giambologna, and others; and the Fountain of Neptune, a masterpiece by Ammannati.

The Uffizi Gallery is one of the most important and impressive museums in Italy, where you can see a vast collection of artworks from the Middle Ages to the Modern period. It is especially famous for its paintings from the 14th-century and Renaissance period, which include some absolute masterpieces by Giotto, Simone Martini, Piero della Francesca, Beato Angelico, Filippo Lippi, Botticelli, Mantegna, Correggio, Leonardo da Vinci, Raphael, Michelangelo, Caravaggio, and many more. You can explore the gallery and its rooms at your own pace or join travellers. You can also visit the Uffizi Library, where you can see books and manuscripts from different periods; or the Uffizi Terrace, where you can enjoy a panoramic view of Florence.

Tips and recommendations: Below are some tips and recommendations to make your trip more enjoyable and affordable:

The best time to visit Florence and the Uffizi Gallery is from April to June or from September to October when the weather is mild and sunny. However, avoid going on weekends or public holidays, when the sites can be crowded and noisy.

Wear comfortable shoes, sunscreen, a hat, sunglasses, and water when visiting Florence and the Uffizi Gallery, as the sites are large and exposed to the sun. You can also bring your food or buy snacks at the vending machines inside the sites.

The entrance fee to Florence is free, but you may have to pay a small fee to enter some of its attractions. The entrance fee to the Uffizi Gallery is €20, but you can visit it for free with a Roma Pass or on the first Sunday of every month. You can also book your tickets online or at the ticket office to avoid long queues.

Conclusion

In this travel guide, we have provided you with some information and tips on how to plan your trip and what to see and do in Rome. We have covered some of the most popular and iconic attractions in Rome, such as the Colosseum, the Vatican City, the Pantheon, the Trevi Fountain, and the Spanish Steps. We have also introduced you to some of the less-known but equally fascinating attractions in Rome, such as the Naples Underground, the Villa Farnesina, the Aventine Hill, and the Tiber River. We have also suggested some day trips to some of the most beautiful and interesting destinations near Rome, such as Ostia Antica, Tivoli, Naples, Pompeii, and Florence.

We hope that this travel guide has helped you to prepare for your trip and to enjoy your time in Rome. We hope that you discover some new aspects and perspectives of Rome that you may not have known before. We hope that you experience some unforgettable moments and memories in Rome that you will cherish forever.

We hope that you fall in love with Rome as much as we have. Have a wonderful time in Rome!

Printed in Great Britain
by Amazon

39742794R00099